LITTLE BOOK OF

ABBA

LITTLE BOOK OF
ABBA

First published in the UK in 2007

© G2 Entertainment Limited 2014

www.G2ent.co.uk

Printed and bound in Europe

ISBN 978-1-782812-46-3

Contents

04   Introduction

16   Formation

20   Fame And The Eurovision Song Contest

32   Benny Andersson

42   Björn Ulvaeus

52   Agnetha Fältskog

62   Anni-Frid Lyngstad

72   Stig Anderson

82   The ABBA Name

84   The Music – Albums And Singles

110   The Money

114   The Music Lives On – ABBA Revival

118   Björn Again – A Tribute

128   Mamma Mia! – The Stage Show

138   Thank You For The Music

Introduction

ABBA-mania first took on a global dimension on 6 April 1974 when the Swedish pop group consisting of Benny Andersson, Björn Ulvaeus, Agnetha Fältskog and Anni-Frid Lyngstad won the Eurovision Song Contest in Brighton. *Waterloo*, with its catchy tune, European flavour and universal lyrics, was the song that launched their international career when they won that night. But it wasn't just the catchy song, the good looks of the band members, their outlandish costumes (which are still a strong theme in Eurovision today) or the love interest between musicians and singers that were to win through; it was the sheer determination of manager Stig Anderson that was to set ABBA on the road to fame and international stardom.

It all began for ABBA in June 1966, when Björn and Benny met at a party. Björn was a member of the Hootenanny Singers while Benny was an up-and-coming performer with the Hep Stars. The Hootenanny Singers were a studio-based group who released their records on Polar Music, which was formed and owned by Stig Anderson and his long-time friend Bengt Bernhag. Björn and Benny were both already successful musicians in their own right, and with Stig Anderson's help they were about to conquer the world. But a songwriting duo – who co-wrote their first song in 1966 – weren't about to do it on their own.

Both men met their future partners – professionally and musically – in the spring of 1969. Benny met Anni-Frid (Frida) while both were performing in a Swedish festival and Björn met Agnetha around the same time. The women were about to become stars' fiancées and the other, all-important half of a phenomenal pop group.

Agnetha and Björn married in 1971, but Benny and Frida managed to wait another seven years before they tied the knot. In the beginning, ABBA didn't exist in the way that the world would see them. The four collaborated on songs written by Benny and Björn

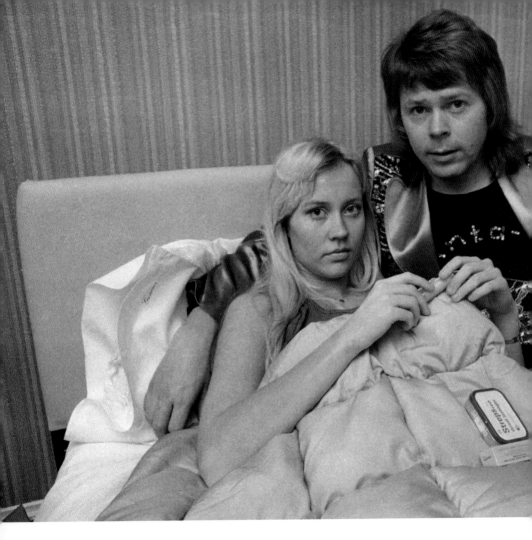

while Agnetha and Frida contributed backing vocals. Stig Anderson was often involved and instrumental in the lyrics – something he was already renowned for in Sweden – and many of the first songs that came from the group were solos or duets.

The group became known as Festfolk and their first medium-sized hit came in 1972 with *People Need Love*. The record marked the first time the two women had provided the lead vocals and all four members of the band – along with manager Anderson – realised that they might just be on to a winning formula.

Encouraged by their success, the band entered the Swedish heats of the Eurovision Song Contest in 1973 with *Ring Ring*. Although it lacked the feisty style that was to come, it did attract some attention for the band from European countries outside Sweden, where they were increasingly popular. However, *Ring Ring* did not do what Stig Anderson wanted and take the band to the Eurovision Song Contest. In fact, the song trailed in third place, leaving all four band members deeply disappointed.

When Anderson got fed up with naming all four members every time

LEFT Agnetha in bed with a cold, comforted by Björn

he gave an interview or promoted the band in any other way, he decided to change their name to ABBA – an acronym of the four members' first initials. It worked and the name stuck. It was far more practical, buzzing and contemporary than any band name they had had before.

After winning the Eurovision Song Contest in 1974, ABBA would have a huge hit with *Waterloo*, which hit the top spot in the charts all over Europe – although strangely, it never made it to Number 1 in the US. The group's first album following their success in Brighton was cannily also called *Waterloo* and went on to become a huge hit in Sweden.

However, despite coming to international attention by winning Eurovision, the success of that night also had its drawbacks. Eurovision was openly referred to as "a joke" by many of ABBA's would-be audiences and, at first, it proved difficult for the group to be taken seriously. It would take ABBA another 18 months before the world at large really began to sit up and take notice.

The band's third album, *ABBA*, seemed to be the key with its hugely successful single *SOS*. Another song

from the album, *Mamma Mia*, saw ABBA take the hot spot in the UK and Australia. The group from a cold, northern hemisphere country with little daylight were about to create ABBA fever in one of the hottest and sunniest places on the planet. The Australians absolutely loved ABBA. They went wild for them and ABBA fever shook Australia for six years.

By 1976, ABBA were firmly established as one of the most popular groups in the world. The same year saw the group release different greatest hits compilations in both the UK and Australia; in the UK it was *ABBA's Greatest Hits* while in Australia they released *The Best Of ABBA*. *Fernando* and *Dancing Queen* – the latter with lyrics by Stig Anderson – both topped the charts in many countries across the globe and, in April 1977, *Dancing Queen* became the group's only US Number 1.

A fourth album, *Arrival*, released in 1976, was aptly named as it coincided neatly with the group's dominance of the world stage. Proving just how popular ABBA were, the album stormed up the charts with hits including *Money, Money, Money* and *Knowing Me, Knowing You*.

LEFT
Smiles and
sunglasses, 1976

Next for ABBA came a successful 1977 tour of Europe and Australia that played to sell-out venues with screaming audiences – which would bother Agnetha – at every concert they gave.

It was also the year when ABBA began work on a feature film, *ABBA – The Movie*, which premiered in December 1977 to coincide with the release of a fifth album, *ABBA – The Album*.

Memorable numbers from the album included *Take A Chance On Me* and *The Name Of The Game*.

The following year saw ABBA take to the stage in the US, where they reached Number 3 with *Take A Chance On Me* and made it into the Top 20 album charts with *ABBA – The Album*. The singles *Chiquitita* and *Summer Night City* were followed by *Voulez-Vous*, the band's sixth album which was released in April 1979.

But all was not well with Björn and Agnetha, who had previously announced their impending divorce while agreeing to stay with the band. This did nothing to help ABBA's image of two loving couples happily making music for a worldwide audience.

In the autumn of 1979, *Gimme! Gimme! Gimme! (A Man After Midnight)* was released and it was immediately followed by a major tour of Canada, the US and Europe. The second compilation album was also released around this time and it provided another massive hit for the group. In March 1980, ABBA toured Japan and followed up by recording their next album, *Super Trouper*, with the title track and *The Winner Takes it All* reaping success in the singles charts.

The following year it looked as if ABBA were on a downward spiral as Benny and Frida announced that they too were heading for a divorce. Despite the emotional turmoil going on within the band, the four members continued to work together and *The Visitors* – their eighth album – was released. *One Of Us*, taken from the album, proved to be a huge hit but the strain of working with ex-partners was, by now, taking its toll.

In 1982, Benny and Björn announced they would be concentrating their efforts on writing a musical, *Chess*, in collaboration with Sir Tim Rice. Stig Anderson firmly believed that they would be back, but he was to be proved wrong. Agnetha and Frida were pursuing solo careers and it looked unlikely that ABBA, as it had been, would ever be the same again.

The group released *The Singles – The First Ten Years* and then decided to take a "break". It has turned out to be one of the longest breaks in history and today, fans, music critics and the world at large recognise the fact that ABBA are extremely unlikely to perform together again. Even in 2014, however, the rumours of a reunion keep resurfacing.

Formation

RIGHT Relaxed
in the '70s

When Frida recorded *Peter Pan* – co-written by Benny and Björn – in 1969 it brought together the first three members of the band that were to become known as ABBA. Benny provided the keyboards on the original recording and Stig Anderson, who had already provided lyrics for songs in Frida's solo career, was hovering in the background. The collaboration between Benny, Björn, Frida and Anderson was already well under way.

Then came Agnetha, and the four musicians began working on an album for a cabaret show called *Festfolket*. They gave their first performance together on a Swedish radio show, *Våra Favoriter*, on 3 October 1970. The show also featured the artists performing their own songs.

The cabaret show went on tour across Sweden in early 1971, but the two couples almost ended their collaboration there and then. It was not a happy experience for the four musicians, who found the tour gruelling and exhausting.

Any plans they may have had of working together as a foursome were quickly fading, and Frida left the three other members of the group to go on tour with Lars Berghagen, the Swedish singer and songwriter with whom she already had an established professional relationship. A duet by Frida and Berghagen subsequently entered the Swedish charts.

LEFT At the airport, 1974

Although plans to work together as a foursome had been shelved, Benny, Björn, Agnetha and Frida still worked on each others' recordings. The first time they recorded together was when Agnetha and Frida provided the backing vocals for Benny and Björn's album *Hej Gamle Man!* And when Frida went on to release her first chart-topper, *Min Egen Stad*, in 1971, the backing vocals were provided by Benny, Björn and Agnetha.

At the end of 1971 and into the early part of 1972, renewed collaboration between the four musicians began to grow. It was fitting that Frida's last solo single for EMI included an A-side written by Benny and Björn, with lyrics for the B-side provided by Stig Anderson. Benny produced the single and provided backing vocals along with Björn and Agnetha.

From then on in, the four of them began to work together regularly and their time on the world stage was about to begin in the guise of ABBA.

Fame And The Eurovision Song Contest

Stig Anderson was instrumental in ABBA's success at the Eurovision Song Contest in 1974. Anderson had prepared the group meticulously for the event and he saw Eurovision as the key to ABBA's breakthrough in the international arena.

It may have been unheard of for a Swedish group to win the contest, but Anderson believed that he, and ABBA, had the recipe for success. He had four great-looking performers who were all close friends and there was also the love interest in that the band was formed of two couples.

At this point, Björn and Agnetha were parents to one-year-old Linda. They also had a magical appeal with their harmonious and instant 'feelgood' music which, combined with their glitzy costumes, gave them glamour and sparkle. The charts of the early 1970s were full of artists in outlandish gear, including Gary Glitter, David Bowie, Marc Bolan, Alice Cooper, Elton John and Alvin Stardust to name but a few.

Although there was some feeling – a feeling that remains – that Eurovision was a bit of a joke and not something that should be taken very seriously, Anderson was convinced that it was the right vehicle to promote his energetic group. The contest had proved time and again that any winning song would be instantly propelled to the top of the European charts while the winning performers

would become overnight stars.

The year before, ABBA had entered the Swedish finals for Eurovision with *Ring Ring*, which had brought them instant success in their homeland. There was a national outcry when the band was not selected by the panel of judges and young and talented singer Lena Anderson was sent to represent Sweden instead. Such was the furore that the selection process for 1974 was changed so that ABBA could take the competition by storm. The major factor that gave the band a landslide victory over their competitors was that the Swedish public were allowed to vote for the act they deemed most likely to win Eurovision. As with *Ring Ring* the previous year, *Waterloo* was believed to have what it would take to bring home the honours.

Waterloo, originally entitled *Honey Pie*, was the song that the Swedish public wanted the rest of Europe to hear. The press – who couldn't get enough of the group – added to the hype and ABBA became a domestic phenomenon with Stig Anderson, the exceptional entrepreneur that he was, keeping the bandwagon

LEFT ABBA meeting at Waterloo

RIGHT Happy
in the park
after Eurovision
success

FAME AND THE EUROVISION SONG CONTEST

rolling. *Waterloo* went on to top the Scandinavian charts and Anderson began his campaign further afield in other European countries including Denmark, where the group became particularly popular.

Wherever possible, demo tapes were sent to sway opinion on the forthcoming contest, while Anderson released pictures of the band as far and as wide as necessary. Some documentaries have even claimed that stickers with the word 'Waterloo' appeared on walls in various places – including Brighton, where the contest would be held. On the day of the 1974 Eurovision contest, ABBA stickers were apparently everywhere, with the result that people began to take this little-known Swedish band seriously.

The title of the song was eventually chosen by Stig Anderson, who had predicted that a catchy name would work wonders. *Honey Pie* was abandoned in favour of his preferred choice, *Waterloo*, which Anderson and the band felt had a winning European flavour – although there were some concerns over which way the French voting would go – and the song had

some relevance to a large audience across the continent.

Waterloo had taken time to materialise. Anderson, Benny and Björn had spent many hours working on the number to ensure that it was exactly right for the voting countries across Europe. On 6 April 1974, ABBA found themselves up against Olivia Newton-John, representing the UK with *Long Live Love*, Anne-Karine Strom from Norway, Holland's Mouth & McNeal and Irene Sheer, representing the previous year's winning country Luxembourg – who were loath to win again because they said they couldn't afford to host another Eurovision.

However, the bookies' original price of 20-1 for ABBA to win the contest started to fall as opinion veered towards the Swedish group, despite Olivia Newton-John's popularity as the 7-2 favourite. In addition, Ireland was a popular choice with their performer, Tina, and her song *Cross Your Heart*.

The Brighton Dome in the rain-swept south east was the venue that was set to host the competition that night and the band were understandably nervous. This was their chance to make

the big time and an entire nation was expecting them to achieve the almost unthinkable – to win. Agnetha had literally been sewn into her costume and she was feeling uncomfortable and, perhaps, a little bit vulnerable.

The live show, with its seventeen competitors, was watched by more than 500 million people in thirty-two countries. ABBA's conductor was Sven-Olof Waldoff, who was dressed like Napoleon Bonaparte – unusual for a conductor who was usually seen in tails – and ABBA were dressed in tight-fitting costumes that left little to the imagination. Indeed, Agnetha's costume was to trigger a worldwide fascination with her bottom that would last throughout her career! With hosts Katie Boyle and Terry Wogan, ABBA took to the Brighton stage and prepared to set the world, let alone Europe, alight.

As soon as Waldoff brought his baton into play, ABBA launched into the performance the audience wanted to hear. It was immediately clear to all concerned that there was no contest between the band from Sweden and the other competitors. ABBA gave an outstanding performance that brought the house down.

The song was an instant success with its bouncy catchiness and in a split second, the drabness of the previous acts had been obliterated by the new Scandinavian sensation. And when the following acts had done their bit, the scores quickly began to tell their own story. A landslide victory was clearly ABBA's.

The elation for the four band members, Anderson and Waldoff was witnessed with delight by the watching millions before ABBA jumped on to the stage for the finale. *Waterloo* had provided a fresh approach to Eurovision that was much needed and had been longed for by organisers and fans alike. No wonder it was a landslide victory.

Following the after-show party and the celebrations back at the hotel, which included copious amounts of champagne, the reality started to sink in. Waterloo went on to take the Number 1 spot at the top of the pop charts across the globe. It would mean that ABBA would be forever linked with Eurovision, but at that time the band didn't care. This instant stardom on an international playing field was

LEFT Ireland's Tina, another popular entry

what they had worked for, what they had strived for. But whether it was the fact that Eurovision gave them their first international hit, or the fact that they were not from pop's traditional heartlands of the US and Britain, ABBA's music was never taken seriously, from that moment until they announced they were taking a break some ten years later.

It could also be that, despite their popular appeal, their music didn't attract a serious audience because it was quite simply pop music. It was fresh, it was lively, the performers were energetic with outlandish costumes and the music didn't pretend to be something it wasn't.

ABBA were happy to be performing pop music – it's what they did best. They had a unique style, they weren't dressing their music up as anything else and it had universal appeal. With instantly memorable choruses, some moving ballads and intricate harmonies mixed with exciting rhythms, ABBA became the top pop band of the 1970s and 1980s, while Benny and Björn proved to be among the greatest songwriters of the twentieth century.

Benny Andersson

RIGHT Benny
and Frida, 1974

Göran Bror Benny Andersson was born in Stockholm in Sweden on 16 December 1946. The exceptional composer and performer has enjoyed a remarkable career since he first joined the Swedish group the Hep Stars.

His father, Gösta Andersson, was a construction worker and Benny had a younger sister, Eva-Lis, who was born two years after him in 1948. Both his father and grandfather were musical and played the accordion and presented the young Benny, then aged six, with his own instrument. He learnt Swedish folk music – taught by both his father and grandfather – as well as traditional music, but he was heavily influenced by the 'King' of rock 'n' roll, Elvis Presley.

Aged ten, Benny taught himself to play the piano and when he left school at fifteen he began performing in youth clubs, where he met Christina Grönvall. The couple had two children, Peter (born 1963) and Helen (born 1965). In 1964, Benny and Christina joined the Electricity Board Folk Music Group, whose music consisted mainly of instrumentals including the number *Baby Elephant Walk*, written by Benny.

It was around this time that he began writing his own songs which the band were more than happy to perform. The group found themselves up against the Hep Stars in a talent contest in March 1964, and Benny took over as the competitor band's keyboard player later that year. Playing for the Hep Stars, he realised that he wanted a career as a professional musician.

Benny didn't have to wait long for a taste of success with his new band. Their breakthrough came in March 1965 with the hit *Cadillac*. It was to lead to a successful career and the Hep Stars became one of Sweden's most celebrated pop bands during the 1960s. Benny found himself as a driving force for the band and his own material – *No Response*, *Wedding*, *Consolation*, *Sunny Girl*, *She Will Love You* and *It's Nice To Be Back*, to name but a few – proved

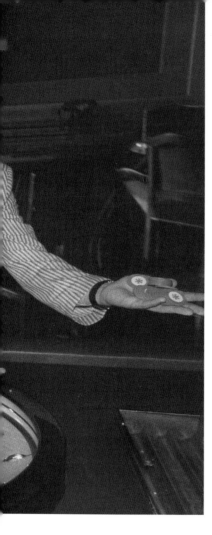

popular with the fans. But despite Benny's songwriting abilities, the band also continued to perform cover versions of many international hits as these gave them more of a following.

It was Benny's chance meeting with the Hootenanny Singers on a road just outside Ålleberg, while travelling with the Hep Stars, that was to change his fortunes for ever. The Hep Stars were invited to a party later that night and it was here that Benny was to meet Björn Ulvaeus. The year was 1966 and after a successful party – at which both bands played songs by the Beatles – Benny and Björn found that they were ideally suited to working together. Their first collaboration was *Isn't It Easy To Say*, which the Hep Stars recorded. But Björn wasn't the only musician with whom Benny was working.

He had an established writing partnership with Lasse Berghagen and the two songwriters wrote a number of popular numbers together, including *Hey, Clown* for the Swedish Eurovision Song Festival. The song made it to the finals of the competition in 1969 and finished in second place.

The festival, however, wasn't just

LEFT ABBA taking a chance

BENNY ANDERSSON

RIGHT Benny, Frida and Björn

going to prove successful musically; it was to prove meaningful on a personal level too. At the festival, Benny met Anni-Frid Lyngstad, who was also participating, and they soon became a couple. At around the same time, Björn met Agnetha. The four friends then became very close as their friendships blossomed and their music looked as if it could reach the big time with Benny's and Björn's continued writing collaboration.

Ljuva Sextiotal and *Speleman* were hits for Brita Borg and the Hep Stars respectively, but the voices of Agnetha and Anni-Frid (Frida) were beginning to convince Benny and Björn that their own group could follow in the footsteps of acts such as the Sweet and Blue Mink among others. ABBA was a fledgling band that was about to take the world by storm.

Benny enjoyed eleven successful years with ABBA before the foursome split in 1982. The ABBA years resulted in seven studio albums, global success and a run of Number 1 hits. But his career was far from over following the decline of ABBA. Even though Benny and Björn were unable to read music,

their partnership continued and further collaboration saw the musical, *Chess*, unveiled in front of both London and Broadway audiences.

The album of music from *Chess* was released in 1984 with vocals by Elaine Paige, Barbra Dickson – including the hit single *I Know Him So Well* – Murray Head, Tommy Körberg and Björn Skifswas. The album was a huge success and sold more than two million copies worldwide. *I Know Him So Well* became a huge Number 1 hit and *One Night In Bangkok*, sung by Murray Head, made it to Number 3 in the US charts.

The Prince Edward Theatre in London's West End was home to the musical for three years between May 1986 and 1989. But when the show opened on Broadway in 1988, despite two successful years in London, it was panned by the critics and closed after only two months.

Meanwhile, Benny produced and released an album in 1985 with Swedish vocalists Anders and Karin Glenmark (a brother and sister duo who had added many vocals to recordings on *Chess*). The Benny and Björn collaboration was as strong as ever and, under the name of Gemini, the Glenmarks released a second collaboration in 1987 from the former ABBA songwriters, their old friends. One of the biggest hits to come out of the album was *Mio My Mio*.

The same year would also see Benny release his first solo album, *Chime, My Bells*, which featured all his own material and the man himself playing the accordion. Two years later, in November 1989, he was back with a second album.

By this time, Benny had already been working on another idea that centred around a Swedish musical based on traditional folk music. In October 1995, *Kristina Frän Duvemåla*, a musical written with Björn, premiered in their home country. Based on the novels of Swedish writer Vilhelm Moberg, the show opened to critical acclaim and ran for five years. There is still some hope that an English version will make it to Broadway.

Next came the musical *Mamma Mia!*, which features twenty-four original ABBA songs. With a play written by the talented Catherine Johnson and the music produced by Björn and overall production by Judy Craymer, the stage show was assured of great success. The musical became a huge phenomenon

LEFT Benny and his wife, Mona Nörklit

on both sides of the Atlantic and Benny worked on re-recording the ABBA songs for the movie version of the musical, which hit the big screen in July 2008. Starring Meryl Streep, Pierce Brosnan, Colin Firth and Stellan Skarsgård, *Mamma Mia* went on to become the highest-grossing musical film of all time, and there is even talk of a sequel.

Benny still enjoys performing and plays with his own band, the Benny Andersson Orkester, or BAO! for short. The band even plays songs with lyrics written by Björn from time to time while the sixteen-piece orchestra supports vocalists Helen Sjöholm and Tommy Körgberg. In April 2007, the band beat a Swedish record when the song *Du Är Min Man* (You Are My Man) stayed in the charts for 143 weeks.

Songs and performing are not Benny's only forte though; he is also a prolific film composer. His first film score came in the early 1970s with *The Seduction Of Inga*. *She's My Kind Of Girl* from the original soundtrack made it to Number 1 in Japan under the title *The Little Girl Of The Cold Wind*. But it was to be several years before Benny once again tackled a film score. The result, in

1987, was *Mio In The Land Of Faraway*, whose story is based around the Swedish author Astrid Indgrens Mio.

In 2000, Benny wrote the music for Roy Andersson's *Songs From The Second Floor* and the music was later re-recorded by BAO!.

After the longest engagement in history, Benny and Frida finally married in 1978, but the engagement was to prove longer than the marriage. The couple were divorced just one year after Björn and Agnetha. Benny then married Mona Nörklit and their son Ludvig was born in 1982.

Following his time with ABBA, Benny won four Swedish Grammys and received the Ivor Novello Award from the British Academy of Composers and Songwriters together with his long-term collaborator Björn. He also won the Music Export Prize from the Swedish Government as well as a Lifetime Achievement Award from the Swedish Music Publishers Association (SMFF). In 2002, Benny Andersson was awarded an honorary professorship by the Swedish government for his "ability to create high-class music reaching people around the world".

Björn Ulvaeus

Björn Kristian Ulvaeus, sometimes described as the most talented member of ABBA, was born in Gothenburg on 25 April 1945. His family soon moved to Västervik, where he went on to study business, economics and law at the University of Lund after completing his military service.

But music was Björn's passion, and he joined Mackie's Skiffle Group, which had been formed by two former schoolmates, Hansi Schwarz and Johan Karlberg. Along with another friend, Tony Rooth, the group performed at parties and schools. They even entered amateur contests before travelling across Europe in an old Volvo, making some money by busking.

By 1962, the group had begun concentrating on folk music and changed their name to the West Bay Singers. Björn decided to enter the group in the *Plats På Scen*, an amateur national talent competition. The exposure brought the young band to the attention of Stig Anderson and his partner, record producer Bengt Bernhag, who had just formed the Polar Music record label.

West Bay Singers were asked to send in a demo tape to the music company, who decided upon hearing the band's numbers to sign them to their label. On the advice of Stig Anderson and Bernhag, the group changed their name to the Hootenanny Singers and entered a talent show, singing in Swedish. This was unusual for bands of the time, for they were used to singing in English. Whether this helped or not, the band won the contest with *Jag Vänter Vid Min Mila*. The song was released as a single and became a hit for the Hootenanny Singers and for the fledgling Polar Music.

In 1964, the band members sat and passed their final school exams, which left them free to follow a professional career in music. Their next big hit came with *Gabrielle* later that year and by the end of 1964, the Hootenanny Singers were a major success across Sweden. To coincide with a national folk tour,

the group released two albums, both of which were called *Hootenanny Singers*.

The following year saw them release an album as a tribute to the renowned Swedish songwriter Evert Taube. *Hootenanny Singer Sjunger Evert Taube* did well across their fan base, but the group were desperate to change their style. Björn, of all the members of the band, was particularly keen to find a way into the more desirable pop scene. The former American hootenanny music that had greatly influenced their music up to this point became less and less important as the group veered towards a more British style, influenced especially by the Beatles.

For the second album in 1965, Björn wrote two new compositions, *Time To Move Along* and *No Time*, while the album *International* also included what was to become a major hit for the band – *Björkens Visa*. The years 1964 to 1966 saw the release of singles in the UK, US, France, Belgium, Denmark, Germany, Italy and the Netherlands as well as Norway and Spain – but it didn't prove to be a particularly successful time.

However, the band scored a massive hit with *No Time* in South Africa and one of the band's B-sides, *Baby Those Are The Rules*, written by Björn, was a success on home territory. Moderate success abroad was followed by another album, *Många Ansikten* (Many Faces), and the A-side *Marianne* provided another hit for the group.

National Service was mandatory for Rooth, Karlberg and Björn. As a German citizen, Schwarz was not subject to the demands of National Service but the other three members of the band all joined the Lifeguards in June 1966. The day before their service was due to begin, the Hootenanny Singers met the Hep Stars just outside Ålleberg and told the successful contemporary group about a farewell party that evening. Benny and Björn met that night and began the long-term partnership that would see them become producers for Polar Music, members of ABBA and co-writers of three globally successful musicals. Their partnership is still strong today.

The summer of 1966 saw Benny and Björn compose their first song together, *Isn't It Easy To Say*. Unlike the three members of the Hootenanny Singers, the Hep Stars had been granted

BJÖRN ULVAEUS

RIGHT Star
and guitar, 1974

leave from National Service as their musical contribution to Sweden was considered more important. After finishing his National Service, Björn went to university and decided to work at Polar Music in his spare time so that he could learn more about the music profession. It was around this time that the group's album *Civilians* was released, and it contained a number of cover versions of US country and folk songs based on the same sort of style as Tom Jones's *Green, Green Grass Of Home*. This particular song from the popular stalwart provided one of the biggest hits that the Hootenanny Singers would have, in January 1967.

Björn's first solo single came in 1968, when he released *Raring*. At this point, he seemed to be the only member of the band that thought that a career in pop music was still possible. Another single, *Fröken Fredriksson*, also became a hit for the newly found soloist. Both the first two singles were covers of US hits, but the B-sides were Björn's own compositions.

He was still performing – on tour – with the Hootenanny Singers and releasing records, and the group went on to release two further albums

in 1968. It was also decided, by the other members of the group, that the Hootenanny Singers would abandon all hope of becoming a pop band. Instead, they focused on producing entirely traditional Swedish numbers and released an album that was written as a tribute to Carl Michael Bellman, the eighteenth century Swedish composer.

The following year saw Björn release two more singles, the second of which was co-written with Benny Andersson and was a tongue-in-cheek commentary on the effects of too much partying.

The Best Of The Hootenanny Singers And Björn Ulvaeus was released in 1969, but in the spring, Karlberg left the group to work for his father's company, believing his performing days were over. The group's follow-up album was aptly named *With The Three Of Us*. And, even though there were now only three of them, Björn wanted to follow other pursuits as a stand-alone artist while co-writing material with Benny.

However, the differences didn't seem to make much difference to the Hootenanny Singers. They continued to tour and release new albums – there were new releases in 1970, 1971 and

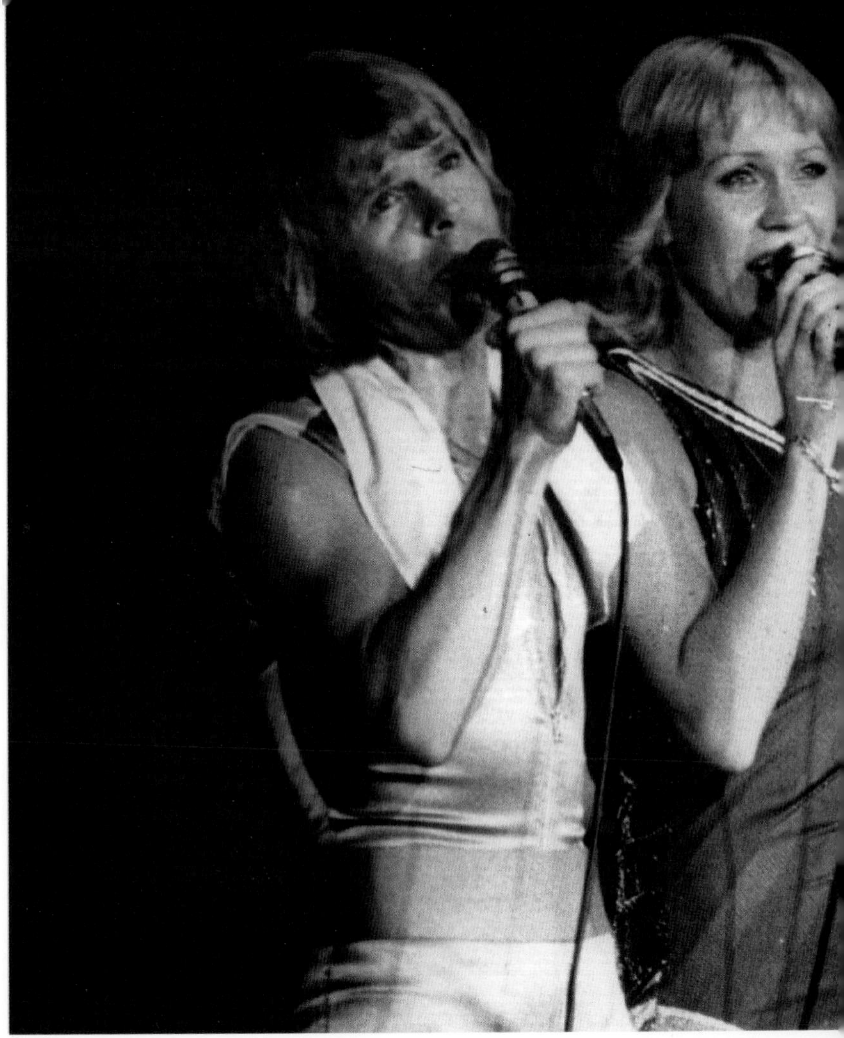

RIGHT Björn sings with the girls, 1979

On a personal level, Björn and Agnetha had two children, Linda (born 1973) and Christian (born 1977).

Another album paying homage to Evert Taube was released by the Hootenanny Singers in 1974 – it was to be the last album that Björn would make with the group. *People Need Love* was the first time that a four-way collaboration between the two couples that formed ABBA took place, and it was to mark a turning point.

That same year was to be instrumental in turning ABBA's fortunes around and Björn found himself concentrating on his new group as the band's faces were splashed across newspapers worldwide when they won the Eurovision Song Contest in April 1974.

After his marriage to Agnetha ended in divorce in 1980, Björn married music journalist Lena Kallersjö on 6 January 1981 and the couple had two daughters, Emma (born 1982) and Anna (born 1986). When ABBA split nine years after their historic Eurovision win, Björn and Benny decided to continue their collaboration by co-writing the musical *Chess*.

RIGHT Björn with his wife, Lena Kallersjö

1972 – but by the following year Björn was busier than ever writing with Benny, while the two women in their respective lives, Agnetha and Anni-Frid (Frida) were contributing more and more to the two men's backing vocals.

Agnetha Fältskog

In April 2004, Agnetha released a single, *If I Thought You'd Ever Change Your Mind*, from the album *My Colouring Book*. It was a comeback after years of living as a recluse since the infamous ABBA split in 1982.

The song, originally a hit for Cilla Black in 1969, was released by Warner to coincide with the thirtieth anniversary of victory at the Eurovision Song Contest in 1974. The company were confident that Agnetha's comeback would revive her career and stated that "the new CD will be one of our biggest releases this year … It's a big deal for us because she's a megastar – a name that everyone knows". A Warner spokesman went on to state of Agnetha: "She has such a distinctive voice that you know who is singing immediately."

Warner had released Agnetha's solo album *Stand Alone* way back in 1987. The fact that the album didn't do well was blamed on poor publicity through lack of promotion. Rumours that money was behind Agnetha's decision

to record again in 2004 were rife when figures suggested in 2002 that she made just £30,000, as opposed to the £4 million fortune that she was supposed to have received when the band split more than twenty years earlier. With the release of the new album it looked as if, for a while at least, Agnetha's days as a recluse were over. She was spotted in a Stockholm club, the Spy Bar, close to the launch date and her very presence caused a stir among the club's clientele.

However, the blonde singer had spent two decades living alone on the tiny and remote island of Ekero, off the coast of the Swedish capital. It is known that, during her time alone, Agnetha suffered from a number of phobias including flying, open spaces, crowds and heights, and she underwent treatment to overcome her difficulties. But, despite her desire to remain private following her fame with ABBA, Agnetha paid to release *My Colouring Book* to relaunch her career.

Known in Sweden as 'Garbo II' – for feeling haunted by her overwhelming

fame during ABBA's heyday – Agnetha confused and baffled those who didn't understand why someone who was almost destroyed by fame and hysteria should want to make a comeback. But there is possibly a simple explanation. Perhaps Agnetha wanted to regain some control and show that she hadn't just faded away into oblivion.

Made up of cover versions of 1960s songs, the new album was nostalgic for the star (and her fans) and marked a return to the period before her rise to fame with ABBA, when she had a

AGNETHA FÄLTSKOG

RIGHT In full
voice on stage

successful solo career.

Born on 4 May 1950 in Jönköping, Agneta (she added the 'h' to her name later) Åse Fältskog was the older daughter of Ingvar and Birgit Fältskog. Her father was the manager of a department store but had a keen interest in music and show business.

Inspired by her father's enthusiasm, Agnetha began a successful career as a solo artist at the age of just eighteen. She clocked up a number of chart singles and had some best-selling albums with romantic songs that were "pretty" and catchy: numbers such as *Som Gladije* (with lyrics by Stig Anderson), *If These Tears Were Gold* and *Mina Ögon*.

Her career had begun when Agnetha, at fifteen years old, joined the local dance band as a vocalist. Her songwriting abilities provided her with a Swedish Number 1 with *I Was So In Love* in 1967. She discovered she had a talent for both writing and performing and went on to establish herself as one of the most popular female vocalists in her home country. In 1968, Agnetha also worked for a time in Germany, where she released singles in German in collaboration with legendary songwriter

Dieter Zimmermann, her fiancé for a short time.

Seven years later – despite being hugely successful with ABBA – Agnetha was continuing with her solo career and in 1975 released the album *Eleven Women In A House*. Several of its songs were described by critics as having a Kate Bush feel.

A year after she met Björn Ulvaeus, Agnetha became romantically involved with the singer/songwriter when they appeared on a Swedish television programme together in 1969. Following their divorce, the couple continued to work together for a further two years before the group split in 1982.

After ABBA decided to "take a break" in the early 1980s, Agnetha went on to release three albums in English. She achieved moderate success in Europe – mainly in Scandinavia – and in the summer of 1982 she made her acting debut in *Raskenstam* – a Swedish movie for which she won praise.

Her first solo album following ABBA came in 1983. *Wrap Your Arms Around Me* was a moderate hit in the US and Australia and made the charts in Scandinavia, selling 1.2 million copies

worldwide. It went to Number 1 in both Denmark and Belgium and hit the Number 2 spot in the Netherlands. But it received a mixed critical reaction, with *Rolling Stone* magazine claiming that the "treacly ... outing doesn't do [Agnetha] justice ...", while *Stereo Review* disagreed and stated that it was "highly entertaining". But mixed reviews shouldn't have worried the star, who received a Best Female Artist award back home in Sweden.

Two years later, *Eyes Of A Woman* was released but it failed to reach the same heights as her previous album. *I Stand Alone* was released by Warner in 1987 but didn't do as well as expected, although in Sweden it spent eight weeks at the top of the charts. Produced by Peter Cetera and Bruce Gaitsch, it became a minor hit in Europe and sold 500,000 copies worldwide.

Agnetha disappeared from public view in 1988 to retreat to her island. It was well known that, of all the members of ABBA, Agnetha was the one who most hated the fame and hysteria that followed the group wherever they went. Despite her musical talents, she would have been just as at home, and

LEFT Agnetha on stage, 1979

AGNETHA FÄLTSKOG

RIGHT Happy
after winning
Eurovision, 1974

just as happy, remaining a housewife bringing up her two children, Linda and Christian. Agnetha hated the touring side of the business, which was often gruelling, and she was often physically sick before going on stage. Her phobia of crowds came about because of the masses of shouting, hysterical fans who surrounded her. Her experiences drove a fear into her and she says in *As I Am,* her autobiography published in 1996: "There's a very thin line between an ecstatic roar and aggressive screaming. It marks your character and turns into phobias."

For the sake of ABBA, Agnetha and Björn claimed that their divorce was amicable. As is so often the case, it was anything but. So it was with a great deal of relief that she turned her back on show business when she moved to Ekero, craving silence. For ten years, Agnetha did not play, sing or listen to music. Her time was spent in more healing pursuits including yoga and alternative medicines. She dated Lars Ericksson (the ice hockey star) before teaming up with fashion designer Dick Haakonsson. She later had a relationship with ThorBjörn Brander, the detective

assigned to her after her children received kidnapping threats, but the relationship didn't last. Then in 1990 she married Tomas Sonnenfeld, who was a surgeon. The marriage lasted three years and ended in divorce in 1993.

In 1997, Agnetha met Dutchman Gert van der Graff, who was sixteen years her junior. Even though she knew van der Graff was obsessed with her – and had been for some time – she still allowed herself to begin a relationship with him. In 2000, Agnetha wrote a letter to van der Graff telling him that she wished to be alone and that there was no hope for the two of them. The obsessed Dutchman was charged with threatening behaviour following the letter.

The relationship ended in legal action and van der Graff was deported – but he returned to Sweden a year later. The police stepped up their surveillance of him when Agnetha returned to the limelight by making a comeback.

The relationship had done nothing to enhance Agnetha's image. Whereas before she took up with van der Graff the Swedish public had felt sympathy for the former star, she was now perceived

AGNETHA FÄLTSKOG

RIGHT
Agnetha on film,
1982

to have acted weirdly by embarking on a relationship with someone who was renowned for being obsessed with her. In court, it emerged Agnetha had admitted to having a relationship with her obsessive fan, whereas before she had convincingly denied any involvement with the Dutchman.

After announcing that she was to make a comeback, Agnetha received an ominous letter that was taken seriously by Swedish police as a death threat. Despite the presence of her own in-house security team, she was assigned a twenty four-hour guard and bodyguards were flown to her home to protect her.

Although Agnetha cultivated her mysterious image to some extent, it is known that she craves affection and a normal life. Very much her own woman, she still wants to prove that she has got what it takes, but on her own terms. Unfortunately, the publicity that surrounds a megastar making a public return to the limelight is bound to produce a considerable amount of attention. That's the name of the game, but the beautiful and talented Agnetha doesn't like playing by all the rules – and why should she?

Anni-Frid Lyngstad

RIGHT
At the gaming
table, 1978

Anni-Frid (Frida) Synni Lyngstad was born on 15 November 1945 in Ballangen, near Narvik in Norway. Her mother, Synni Lyngstad, had a relationship with a married German sergeant, Alfred Haase, while the Nazis were occupying Norway during World War II.

It was not an easy beginning for the legendary vocalist, whose mother was stigmatised following her liaison. The anger felt by the small Norwegian community towards anyone who had dared to fraternise with Germans during the occupation was immense. Frida's mother was regularly spat upon and abused for having a German's baby, but there wasn't just the danger of reprisals. There was also a real threat that Anni-Frid could be removed from her mother's care – and at the time that would have been a normal consequence of the situation that Anni-Frid's mother faced.

As a result, Frida and her grandmother, Arntine Lyngstad, were forced to leave their home in 1947.

They eventually settled in a new home in Eskilstuna close to Torshälla on the Swedish side of the border. Her mother remained in Norway, where she worked until she became too ill – probably caused by the abuse she had suffered. She died, aged just 21, from kidney disease soon after arriving in Sweden where she was reunited with her daughter and mother. Alfred Haase had promised to return to Norway after the war, but he didn't keep his promise. He later claimed he had not known of Synni Lyngstad's pregnancy.

Raised by her grandmother, Frida believed her father had died when the naval ship he was on during the war was sunk. However, she was reunited in 1977 with the father she had never seen, when her biography was published in the German teen magazine *Bravo*. Despite that reunion, however, father and daughter are no longer in contact even though Haase pleaded with Frida to resume contact in 2005 through an article in a German magazine.

Despite the cruel twist of fate that started her life, Frida was destined for great things. Encouraged by her grandmother, Frida first sang in public at the age of ten for an event arranged by the Red Cross. By the age of thirteen she was singing professionally for a local dance band in Eskilstuna. She lied and said she was sixteen to get the job and later began a career with Bengt Sardlind's big band, where she fell in love with Ragnar Frederiksson. The couple went on to form the Anni-Frid 4 and later married and had two children, Hans and Liselotte.

Not content with the progress of her professional life, Frida entered a number of local talent contests – which she won – and competed in the prestigious SVT's Hyland's Corner. Victory in the competition gave her the opportunity to sign for EMI aged twenty-one, but that signing was a surprise as a result of the contest. This part of the prize for winning the 'Nya Ansikten' (New Faces) contest had been kept from the contestants. Despite the prestigious win and the EMI contract, success eluded Frida and it wasn't until she met Benny Andersson in 1969 that her fortunes would change.

Her first single and those that followed over the next three years were not a commercial success for Frida or EMI. A couple made it to the lower regions of the radio charts but none did well on the sales chart. However, the press loved Frida and she received a great deal of airplay, although it did nothing to make her a household name.

There was a great deal of sophistication in Frida's voice and lack of chart success didn't mean that she wasn't good enough to make it as a solo artist. Her voice was natural and relaxed, but perhaps the type of songs she was releasing weren't doing her any favours. Whatever it was, the mix wasn't right and Frida lacked the recognition she craved.

Things began to change in 1969, when she found herself in joint fourth place at the Swedish finals to represent her adopted home country at the Eurovision Song Contest. Between 1968 and 1970, Frida's musical career was taken up by Swedish folkpark venues (a mixture of indoor and outdoor dancehall venues) as well as cabaret. In the autumn of 1969 her collaboration with Benny Andersson on her seventh single, *Peter Pan*, was to lead to a long-

LEFT In a cobbled street, 1975

ANNI-FRID LYNGSTAD

term relationship on both professional and personal levels.

Exactly twelve months after *Peter Pan*, following three years and eight singles for EMI, Frida and Benny began work on her debut album, *Frida*. It was to prove a high point of her years with EMI. Her version of the co-written Benny and Björn song *Lycka*, with lyrics by Stig Anderson, was to prove a highly emotive and personal rendition of what was, in effect, an extremely simple song. She proved she had passion, talent, grit and determination. Her style was unique and soulful.

Benny became Frida's producer, lover and eventually her fiancé when her marriage to Frederiksson broke down. She continued her solo career – through the early ABBA years – up until 1975.

The solo career she had desperately longed for was revived when ABBA began their extended break in 1982. Phil Collins became her producer and at the end of 1982 she released *Something's Going On*. The album reached Number 18 in the UK album charts, although its title track reached a disappointing Number 44.

Shine was released two years later – it was to be Frida's second and

final English album – but it didn't do as well as the first. It proved to be a disappointing time for Frida who decided that – after the album peaked at Number 68 in the UK charts for just one week – she was going to continue her career back in Sweden.

The music industry in Scandinavia and the audiences she recorded for were much more accepting of her individual style than the UK and the rest of Europe had been. Frida enjoyed a successful time, in which she began to contribute to the work of environmental groups. Then, in a surprise move, Frida announced in 1999 that she would no longer be part of the music industry. She stated that she would not record an album or single or sign a record contract ever again.

Today, Frida still lives in her adopted country of Switzerland. She moved there in the mid-1980s and married her long-term boyfriend, Prince Heinrich Ruzzo Reuss, on 26 August 1992. When she married, Frida received the title Her Serene Highness Princess Anni-Frid Reuss of Plauen. Her husband died in 1999 of lymphoma and it was the second tragedy for Frida in two years.

LEFT Thumbs up, 1974

Her daughter Liselotte had died in a fatal car crash in the US in 1998.

Frida's time in Switzerland is spent in charity work, including drug prevention. In an interview with a Dutch women's magazine, Frida showed her forward-thinking, philosophical side when she stated: "I am a strong woman and that is because I was raised like that. But I don't only feel connected with strong women. I especially want to make myself strong for women who aren't.

"With my music, I want to give them strength to let things go. Things that make you unhappy, things that hold up your development and which prevent you from leading your own life. On my CD I sing about the instinct to survive. That instinct is buried in us, it might be deep inside of you. My message is especially aimed at the ones who would like to, but don't dare. I would say, make something of it. You can do it. I'm sure you can."

In February 2011, a BBC radio programme, *Like An Angel Passing Through My Room*, told the story of writer Chris Green's lifelong admiration for Frida. In a rare interview, the former ABBA singer talked frankly about her life.

Stig
Anderson

RIGHT
ABBA and Stig
Anderson at
the group's
custom-built
recording studio
in Stockholm,
1978

Known for his straight talking and his questioning attitude, Stig Anderson didn't always enjoy an easy relationship with other music bosses and publishers, who felt threatened by him. But Anderson was determined that ABBA would win the 1974 Eurovision Song Contest, and he was also determined that they would break through into the international music scene.

One of his most important ideas that contributed to their success was that, to appeal to a European and then worldwide audience, the band's songs had to be in English. This would prove difficult for Benny and Björn, whose first language was obviously Swedish. However, with Anderson's drive, energy and enthusiasm, the lyrics for *Waterloo* were written and the rest is history.

Born Stig Erik Anderson on 25

January 1931 in Hova, Sweden, he grew up in relative poverty with his mother, Ester Andersson. His mother was a resourceful woman and her son inherited her attitude to life. Anderson took on different kinds of jobs at an early age and was greatly influenced by the old gramophone and six 78rpm records that his mother managed to buy when he was around five years old. He enjoyed singing in front of an audience and as a teenager he frequented local venues with his cheap guitar. The sixteen-year-old Anderson found himself rejected by a girl, which led him to writing a ballad – and *Tivedshambo* (Hambo From Tived), the first of his songs to be recorded later in 1951, was to become one of his best-known.

During the 1950s he made some headway as a singer/songwriter but had taken a job as a teacher to maintain some financial stability for his wife and three children. His first big breakthrough came in 1958, when the Swedish football hero Nacka Skoglund recorded *Vi Hanger Me* (We're Still Here). Anderson's song spent twenty weeks in the charts, peaking at Number 6. He acquired the nickname 'Stikkan', which is how he would be known in his native Sweden for the

ANNI-FRID LYNGSTAD

RIGHT
Brighton, 1974

remainder of his life – outside Sweden he was always known as Stig.

Then, in late 1959, Lill-Babe sang Anderson's *Are You Still In Love With Me, Klas-Göran*, which was produced by his long-time friend Bengt Bernhag – one of Sweden's top record producers. It was recorded as a comedy number against the writer's wishes, but the humour turned out to be its biggest asset and it went on to become one of the country's biggest songs in 1960.

Anderson established his own publishing company, Sweden Music, and he concentrated on importing songs which he would then translate into Swedish. As his empire grew – despite some tough years financially in the early 1960s – Anderson found his niche as a lyricist with cover versions of hits such as *Green, Green Grass Of Home*, *You Don't Have To Say You Love Me*, *Honey* and *The Most Beautiful Girl*, to name a few.

In 1963, Anderson and record producer Bernhag founded Polar Music. The first signing to the label was the Hootenanny Singers featuring, of course, Björn Ulvaeus. The band proved popular throughout the 1960s for Polar and when Björn brought in Benny Andersson,

who was singing with the Hep Stars the songwriting trio of Stig, Björn and Benny was born. The relationships that developed between the three men cultivated a dynamism that brought Stig Anderson his first Swedish Grammy for *Mamma Är Lik Sin Mamma* (Mum Is Just Like Her Mum).

One of the first works written by the trio was *Ljuva Sextital* (The Good Old Sixties), which became a major hit, but the death of Bernhag in the early 1970s saw Björn and Benny join Polar Music as house producers, and they all continued developing their songwriting collaboration.

Anderson was instrumental in ABBA's winning approach to the Eurovision Song Contest and, from the winning night, he concentrated his efforts on raising the band's international profile. This saw his own work as a lyricist in decline as he put more and more time into ABBA's songs and their worldwide promotion. While ensuring that ABBA were moving in the right direction on a global scale, back in Sweden Anderson was building his publishing empire with the acquisitions of many major publishing companies. In the late 1980s,

LEFT Frida arrives at the 2004 Polar Music Prize which was founded by Stig Anderson

ANNI-FRID LYNGSTAD

RIGHT
Swedish Queen
Silvia and Crown
Princess Victoria
arrive at the
Polar Music Prize
award, 2004

he sold Polar Music to PolyGram – later, following a merger, to become part of Universal Music.

By this time, his relationship with ABBA and its former members had started to take a downturn, but it was about to get a whole lot worse for all concerned. Anderson had remained a dominant figure in the band's career and represented their commercial interests and global success through many successful record deals. The mid-1980s revealed that a considerable amount of ABBA's fortune had been lost through mismanagement, unsound investments and high tax demands, which led to a breakdown in relationships with Agnetha, Benny and Björn. It also transpired that Anderson had been taking a percentage of the profits – of which the band was unaware – for many years. ABBA had also only received royalties of three per cent whereas a contract established much earlier on had established royalty fees at nine per cent. It is estimated that Anderson profited to the tune of around €4.5 million.

As a result, members of ABBA submitted a complaint against their former manager with the Stockholm District Court. Agnetha's company,

Agnetha Fältskog Produktion AB, Mono Music AB – Benny Andersson's company – the Swiss investors that Frida had sold her investments to and Björn's company all participated in the complaint, but the lawsuit was eventually settled out of court. Anderson's argument over the lower royalty fee was that a higher fee would only be paid if the group made more records. He claimed it was a prerequisite. If they didn't make new records, and that had already been confirmed by Björn and Benny as impossible, then the three per cent was final. Anderson was hurt and bitter about the legal action taken against him. He had always tried to conduct fair business dealings.

Sadly, the legal action meant that Agnetha, Benny and Björn were unable to remain friends with Anderson although Frida, who had sold her shares in Polar Music long before the troubles began, was able to remain friends with him. Björn did try to re-establish his relationship with Anderson but the former manager refused to take his calls. He felt that he had done absolutely everything he could have done, and more, to ensure that ABBA were instantly recognisable worldwide. He had ensured

they were famous. He had conducted all the deals for them – often this was not easy – and he had invested their money wisely according to his close sources. He felt that he had given them everything and had been more than a manager to them; for him, the legal action was a huge breach of loyalty and friendship. He just couldn't forgive.

Anderson established the Polar Music prize, first awarded in 1992. Major recipients of the award include Bob Dylan, Sir Paul McCartney, Joni Mitchell, Stevie Wonder, Bruce Springsteen and Pink Floyd. Anderson retired during the mid-1990s although, despite having sold Polar Music, he continued to remain active within the company.

Stig Anderson had a heart attack on 12 September 1997 and died at the age of 66. His funeral was broadcast live by Swedish television – an honour usually accorded to statesmen or royalty. Even fourteen years after his death, his influence is still evident in the Swedish music industry. The Stikkan Anderson double CD is a celebration of his lyrics and music, and the music entrepreneur is also celebrated by a bronze bust that sits proudly in a square in his home town of Hova.

The ABBA Name

The acronym ABBA comes from the first initials of the four members of the band: Agnetha, Björn, Benny and Anni-Frid. At first there was some confusion over whether the group could use the name ABBA as it was also the name of a Swedish canned fish company. However, with his usual panache, Stig Anderson concluded a deal with the company and ABBA was born.

Originally, the band had used the name Festfolk, which also meant 'engaged couples' and 'party people', before working under their own first names. Festfolk didn't work for the band and they didn't achieve much success under this name. Equally, using Björn & Benny, Agnetha & Anni-Frid was rather long-winded and it was decided – after some consultation and smooth operating by Anderson – that ABBA was a much more viable option.

The Music —
The Albums
And The Singles

Two of the key ingredients in the music of ABBA – the vocals of Agnetha (soprano) and Frida (mezzo-soprano) – were mixed with a keyboard style that was very much Benny's own. Each and every song featured a strong melody that was interspersed with moments of experimentation, often provided by sound engineer Michael Tretow.

The early 1970s saw the group try a number of styles, but by 1975 they had established a multi-layer effect with pleasing harmonies. In the early 1980s ABBA returned to the more basic productions that had dominated their music a decade earlier – with synthesizers playing a vital role in their unique pop style.

The albums

All tracks were written by Andersson, Ulvaeus unless otherwise stated. All records were produced by Benny Andersson and Björn Ulvaeus unless otherwise stated.

Ring Ring

When the first album was released in Sweden on 26 March 1973, the group weren't even called ABBA. Only after the title track became a hit did the four musicians decide to make their collaboration more permanent. The track listing below is for the first UK release of the album, in 1992.

ABBA
GREATEST
HITS

Side 1
SOS
HE IS YOUR BROTHER
RING RING
ANOTHER TOWN, ANOTHER TRAIN
HONEY HONEY
SO LONG
MAMMA MIA

Side 2
I DO, I DO, I DO, I DO, I DO
PEOPLE NEED LOVE
WATERLOO
NINA PRETTY BALLERINA
BANG-A-BOOMERANG
DANCE (WHILE THE MUSIC STILL
GOES ON
FERNANDO

Track listing

Ring Ring (Anderson, Andersson, Ulvaeus, Neil Sedaka, Phil Cody)
Another Town, Another Train
Disillusion (Fältskog, Ulvaeus)
People Need Love
I Saw It In The Mirror
Nina, Pretty Ballerina
Love Isn't Easy (But It Sure Is Hard Enough)
Me And Bobby And Bobby's Brother
He Is Your Brother
She's My Kind of Girl
I Am Just A Girl (Anderson, Andersson, Ulvaeus)
Rock 'n' Roll Band
Recorded: March 1972 to March 1973, Metronome, Europafilm and KMH Studios, Stockholm
Highest chart position: 1 – Belgium

Waterloo

First released on 4 March 1974, *Waterloo* had begun life in the recording studio in September the previous year. Recording was already well under way before ABBA submitted their entry to the Eurovision Song Contest in 1974. It was the first album released under the name of ABBA.

Track listing

Waterloo (Anderson, Andersson, Ulvaeus)
Sitting In The Palmtree
King Kong Song
Hasta Mañana
(Anderson, Andersson, Ulvaeus)
My Mama Said
Dance (While The Music Still Goes On)
Honey, Honey (Anderson, Andersson, Ulvaeus)
Watch Out
What About Livingstone?
Gonna Sing You My Lovesong
Suzy-Hang-Around
Recorded: September 1973 to January 1974, Metronome Studios, Stockholm
Highest chart position: 1 – Sweden and Norway

ABBA

Following on from Eurovision success, recording sessions began in August 1974 for the third album, which was released on 21 April 1975. The multi-layered sound that became synonymous with the group was firmly established with this album.

Track listing

Mamma Mia (Anderson, Andersson, Ulvaeus)

Hey, Hey Helen
Tropical Loveland (Anderson, Andersson, Ulvaeus)
SOS (Anderson, Andersson, Ulvaeus)
Man In The Middle
Bang-A-Boomerang (Anderson, Andersson, Ulvaeus)
I Do, I Do, I Do, I Do, I Do (Anderson, Andersson, Ulvaeus)
Rock Me
Intermezzo No 1
I've Been Waiting For You (Anderson, Andersson, Ulvaeus)
So Long
Recorded: April 1974 to March 1975, Glen, Metronome and Ljudkopia Studios, Stockholm
Highest chart position: 1 – Sweden, Norway, Australia and Zimbabwe

Greatest Hits

On 17 November 1975, ABBA released their *Greatest Hits* album, the first compilation of many. The song *Fernando* was only included on the album for certain releases during the first few months of 1976.

Track listing

SOS (Anderson, Andersson, Ulvaeus)
He Is Your Brother

Ring Ring (Anderson, Andersson, Cody, Sedaka, Ulvaeus)
Hasta Mañana (Anderson, Andersson, Ulvaeus)
Nina, Pretty Ballerina
Honey, Honey (Anderson, Andersson, Ulvaeus)
So Long
I Do, I Do, I Do, I Do, I Do (Anderson, Andersson, Ulvaeus)
People Need Love
Bang-A-Boomerang (Anderson, Andersson, Ulvaeus)
Another Town, Another Train
Mamma Mia (Anderson, Andersson, Ulvaeus)
Dance (While The Music Still Goes On)
Waterloo (Anderson, Andersson, Ulvaeus)
Highest chart position: 1 – Sweden, Norway, UK and Zimbabwe

Arrival

ABBA's fourth studio album was first released on 11 October 1976 following recording sessions stretching out over a year. It was to spawn some of the group's greatest hits including *Dancing Queen, Money, Money, Money* and *Knowing Me, Knowing You*. This was the album that pushed ABBA's direct pop

RIGHT
Amanda Seyfried
was perfectly
cast as Sophie in
Mamma Mia! The
Movie

style to the limit.

Track listing

When I Kissed The Teacher
Dancing Queen (Anderson, Andersson, Ulvaeus)
My Love, My Life (Anderson, Andersson, Ulvaeus)
Dum Dum Diddle
Knowing Me, Knowing You (Anderson, Andersson, Ulvaeus)
Money, Money, Money
That's Me (Anderson, Andersson, Ulvaeus)
Why Did It Have To Be Me
Tiger
Arrival

Recorded: August 1975 to September 1976, Metronome and Glen Studios, Stockholm

Highest chart position: 1 – Australia, Belgium, Mexico, the Netherlands, New Zealand, Norway, Sweden, UK, West Germany, Zimbabwe

ABBA – The Album

Released on 12 December 1977, this album included a number of longer tracks with more complex musical structures than fans were used to. The album was released to coincide with

ABBA – The Movie, which was showing in cinemas worldwide.

Track listing

Eagle
Take A Chance On Me
One Man, One Woman
The Name Of The Game (Anderson, Andersson, Ulvaeus)
Move On (Anderson, Andersson, Ulvaeus)
Hole In Your Soul
The Girl With The Golden Hair – three scenes from a mini-musical:
Thank You For The Music
I Wonder (Departure) (Anderson, Andersson, Ulvaeus)
I'm A Marionette

Recorded: May to November 1977, Marcus, Metronome and Glen Studios, Stockholm and Bohus Studio, Kungalv

Highest chart position: 1 – Belgium, Mexico, New Zealand, Norway, Sweden, Switzerland, the Netherlands and the UK

Voulez-Vous

Recording began on *Voulez-Vous* in March 1978 and continued for twelve months before it was finally released on 23 April 1979. This sixth album was recorded at a time when the entire world was in the grip of disco fever.

Track listing

As Good As New
Voulez-Vous
I Have A Dream
Angeleyes
The King Has Lost His Crown
Does Your Mother Know
If It Wasn't For The Nights
Chiquitita
Lovers (Live A Little Longer)
Kisses Of Fire

Recorded: Polar Music Studios, Stockholm and Criteria Studios, Miami

Highest chart position: 1 – Argentina, Belgium, Finland, Japan, Mexico, Norway, Sweden, Switzerland, UK, West Germany and Zimbabwe

Greatest Hits Vol 2

The group's second compilation album was released on 29 October 1979. It was essentially a round-up of all the hits since the first compilation record and was released to coincide with ABBA's tour of Europe and the US.

Track listing

Gimme! Gimme! Gimme! (A Man After Midnight)

Knowing Me, Knowing You (Anderson, Andersson, Ulvaeus)
Take A Chance On Me
Money, Money, Money
Rock Me
Eagle
Angeleyes
Dancing Queen (Anderson, Andersson, Ulvaeus)
Does Your Mother Know
Chiquitita
Summer Night City
I Wonder (Departure) (Anderson, Andersson, Ulvaeus)
The Name Of The Game (Anderson, Andersson, Ulvaeus)
Thank You For The Music

Highest chart position: 1 – Belgium, Canada and the UK

Super Trouper

Released on 3 November 1980, *Super Trouper* was recorded between February and October of that year. Björn and Agnetha's divorce, just prior to the album's release, was highlighted in the track *The Winner Takes It All*.

Track listing

Super Trouper
The Winner Takes It All

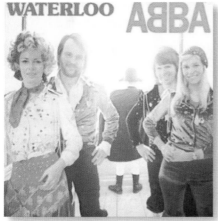

On And On And On
Andante, Andante
Me And I
Happy New Year
Our Last Summer
The Piper
Lay All Your Love On Me
The Way Old Friends Do (live)
Recorded: Polar Music Studios, Stockholm
Highest chart position: 1 – Belgium, Mexico, Norway, Sweden, Switzerland, the Netherlands, UK, West Germany and Zimbabwe

The Visitors

Recordings for the group's eighth album took place between March 1981 and November of that year. It was released on 30 November 1981 and was described by critics as "bleak". A 2012 deluxe edition contained the bonus track *From A Twinkling Star To A Passing Angel.*

Track listing
The Visitors (Crackin' Up)
Head Over Heels
When All Is Said And Done
Soldiers
I Let The Music Speak
One Of Us

Two For The Price Of One
Slipping Through My Fingers
Like An Angel Passing Through My Room
Recorded: Polar Music Studios, Stockholm
Highest chart position: 1 – Belgium, Norway, Sweden, Switzerland, the Netherlands, UK, West Germany and Zimbabwe

The Singles – The First Ten Years

The album was released on 8 November 1982 and marked the end of ABBA's career as a group. Originally, they had planned to record new songs – just as they had done every year – but all four members felt that their energy had gone. This double album was released instead.

Track listing, disc one:
Ring Ring (Anderson, Andersson, Cody, Sedaka, Ulvaeus)
Waterloo (Anderson, Andersson, Ulvaeus)
So Long
I Do, I Do, I Do, I Do, I Do (Anderson, Andersson, Ulvaeus)
*SOS (*Anderson, Andersson, Ulvaeus)
Mamma Mia (Anderson, Andersson, Ulvaeus)
Fernando (Anderson, Andersson, Ulvaeus)
Dancing Queen (Anderson, Andersson,

Ulvaeus)
Money, Money, Money
Knowing Me, Knowing You (Anderson, Andersson, Ulvaeus)
The Name Of The Game (Anderson, Andersson, Ulvaeus)
Take A Chance On Me
Summer Night City
Disc two:
Chiquitita
Does Your Mother Know
Voulez-Vous
Gimme! Gimme! Gimme! (A Man After Midnight)
I Have A Dream
The Winner Takes It All
Super Trouper
One Of Us
The Day Before You Came
Under Attack
Highest chart position: 1 – Belgium, South Africa and the UK

ABBA Live

ABBA fans had demanded a live album for many years. The group had traditionally always been against the idea, but this release finally gave the fans what they wanted, four years after the group had split. It was released in August 1986,

with most of the tracks coming from ABBA's concert at Wembley in 1979, while others came from an Australian tour two years earlier.

Track listing

Dancing Queen (Anderson, Andersson, Ulvaeus)

Take A Chance On Me

I Have A Dream

Does Your Mother Know

Chiquitita

Thank You For The Music

Two For The Price Of One

Fernando (Anderson, Andersson, Ulvaeus)

Gimme! Gimme! Gimme! (A Man After

Midnight)
Super Trouper
Waterloo
Producer: Michael B Tretow
Highest chart position: 49 – Sweden

ABBA Gold

The album was first released on 21 September 1992 and over the years has sold more than twenty-eight million copies worldwide. It is the twenty-eighth best-selling album of all time. It was re-released in 1999 to mark the twenty-fifth anniversary of ABBA's success at the 1974 Eurovision Song Contest, and again in 2002 to mark the album's tenth anniversary.

Track listing
Dancing Queen (Anderson, Andersson, Ulvaeus)
*Knowing Me, Knowing You (*Anderson, Andersson, Ulvaeus)
Take A Chance On Me
Mamma Mia (Anderson, Andersson, Ulvaeus)
Lay All Your Love On Me
Super Trouper
I Have A Dream
The Winner Takes It All
Money, Money, Money

SOS (Anderson, Andersson, Ulvaeus)
Chiquitita
Fernando (Anderson, Andersson, Ulvaeus)
Voulez-Vous
Gimme! Gimme! Gimme! (A Man After Midnight)
Does Your Mother Know
One Of Us
The Name Of The Game (Anderson, Andersson, Ulvaeus)
Thank You For The Music
Waterloo (Anderson, Andersson, Ulvaeus)
Highest chart position: 1 – Australia, Austria, Belgium, Finland, France, Germany, Ireland, Mexico, Norway, Spain, Sweden, Switzerland and the UK

More ABBA Gold

This album was released on 1 June 1993 in Sweden after the original *ABBA Gold*, released the previous year, had stormed up the charts. A surprise inclusion was the previously unreleased song *I Am The City*, which was recorded in one of the group's final recording sessions in 1982.

Track listing
Summer Night City
Angeleyes

The Day Before You Came
Eagle
I Do, I Do, I Do, I Do, I Do (Anderson, Andersson, Ulvaeus)
So Long
Honey, Honey (Anderson, Andersson, Ulvaeus)
The Visitors
Our Last Summer
On And On And On
Ring Ring (Anderson, Andersson, Cody, Sedaka, Ulvaeus)
I Wonder (Departure) (Anderson, Andersson, Ulvaeus)
Lovelight
Head Over Heels
When I Kissed The Teacher
I Am The City
Cassandra
Under Attack
When All Is Said And Done
The Way Old Friends Do
Highest chart position: 2 – Zimbabwe

Thank You For the Music

Twelve years after ABBA split up, this album was released on 31 October 1994. The four-CD collection featured hits, much-loved numbers and previously unreleased songs including an alternative version of *Thank You For The Music*, *Dream World* and a twenty-three-minute medley of other songs never heard before, entitled *ABBA Undeleted*.

Track listing, disc one:
People Need Love
Another Town, Another Train
He Is Your Brother
Love Isn't Easy (But It Sure Is Hard Enough)
Ring Ring (Anderson, Andersson, Cody, Sedaka, Ulvaeus)
Waterloo (Anderson, Andersson, Ulvaeus)
Hasta Mañana (Anderson, Andersson, Ulvaeus)
Honey, Honey (Anderson, Andersson, Ulvaeus)
Dance (While The Music Still Goes On)
So Long
I've Been Waiting For You (Anderson, Andersson, Ulvaeus)
I Do, I Do, I Do, I Do, I Do (Anderson, Andersson, Ulvaeus)
SOS (Anderson, Andersson, Ulvaeus)
Mamma Mia (Anderson, Andersson, Ulvaeus)
Fernando (Anderson, Andersson, Ulvaeus)
Dancing Queen (Anderson, Andersson, Ulvaeus)

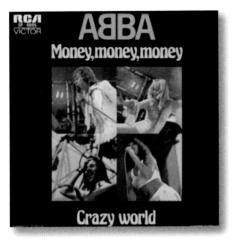

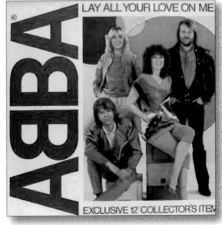

That's Me (Anderson, Andersson,
Ulvaeus)
When I Kissed The Teacher
Money, Money, Money
Crazy World
My Love, My Life (Anderson, Andersson,
Ulvaeus)
Disc two:
Knowing Me, Knowing You (Anderson,
Andersson, Ulvaeus)
Happy Hawaii (Anderson, Andersson,
Ulvaeus)
The Name Of The Game (Anderson,
Andersson, Ulvaeus)

MORE
ABBA
GOLD

MORE ABBA HITS

I Wonder (Departure) (Anderson,
Andersson, Ulvaeus)
Eagle
Take A Chance On Me
Thank You For The Music
Summer Night City
Chiquitita
Lovelight
Does Your Mother Know
Voulez-Vous
Angeleyes
Gimme! Gimme! Gimme!
(A Man After Midnight)
I Have A Dream
Disc three:
The Winner Takes It All
Elaine
Super Trouper
Lay All Your Love On Me
On And On And On
Our Last Summer
The Way Old Friends Do (live)
The Visitors
One Of Us
Should I Laugh Or Cry
Head Over Heels
When All Is Said And Done
Like An Angel Passing Through My Room
The Day Before You Came
Cassandra

Under Attack
Disc four:
Put On Your White Sombrero
Dream World
Thank You For The Music (Doris Day mix)
Hej Gamle Man!
Merry-Go-Round
Santa Rosa
She's My Kind Of Girl
Medley: Pick A Bale Of Cotton
(Traditional, Andersson, Ulvaeus)
You Owe Me One
Slipping Through My Fingers/Me And I (live)
*ABBA Undeleted: Scaramouche/Summer
Night City / Take A Chance On Me /
Baby / Just A Notion / Rikky Rock 'n'
Roller / Burning My Bridges / Fernando*
(Frida Swedish solo version) (Anderson,
Andersson, Ulvaeus) */ Here Comes Rubie
Jamie* (Anderson, Andersson, Ulvaeus)
*/ Hamlet III Parts 1 & 2 / Free As A
Bumble Bee / Rubber Ball Man / Crying
Over You / Just Like That / Givin' a Little
Bit More*
Waterloo (Anderson, Andersson, Ulvaeus)
Ring Ring (Swedish, Spanish, German)
(Anderson, Andersson, Ulvaeus)
Honey, Honey (Swedish) (Anderson,
Andersson, Ulvaeus)
Highest chart position: 17 – Sweden

The Definitive Collection

Released on the 2 November 2001, *The Definitive Collection* is based on the same concept as *The Singles – The First Ten Years*. It includes every track that was recorded and released by Polar Music between 1972 and 1982. There are thirty-seven tracks on the album, with some songs that were not chosen as Polar A-sides at the time of recording. The album also includes a remix of *Ring Ring* and an extended US remix of *Voulez-Vous*.

Track listing, disc one:

People Need Love
He Is Your Brother
Ring Ring (Anderson, Andersson, Cody, Sedaka, Ulvaeus)
Love Isn't Easy (But It Sure Is Hard Enough)
Waterloo (Anderson, Andersson, Ulvaeus)
Honey, Honey (Anderson, Andersson, Ulvaeus)
So Long
I Do, I Do, I Do, I Do, I Do (Anderson, Andersson, Ulvaeus)
SOS (Anderson, Andersson, Ulvaeus)
Mamma Mia (Anderson, Andersson, Ulvaeus)
Fernando (Anderson, Andersson, Ulvaeus)
Dancing Queen (Anderson, Andersson, Ulvaeus)
Money, Money, Money (Anderson, Andersson, Ulvaeus)
Knowing Me, Knowing You (Anderson, Andersson, Ulvaeus)
The Name Of The Game (Anderson, Andersson, Ulvaeus)
Take A Chance On Me
Eagle
Summer Night City
Chiquitita
Does Your Mother Know
Hasta Mañana (Anderson, Andersson, Ulvaeus)

Disc two:

Voulez-Vous
Angeleyes
Gimme! Gimme! Gimme!
(A Man After Midnight)
I Have A Dream
The Winner Takes It All
Super Trouper
On And On And On
Lay All Your Love On Me
One Of Us
When All Is Said And Done
Head Over Heels
The Visitors
The Day Before You Came

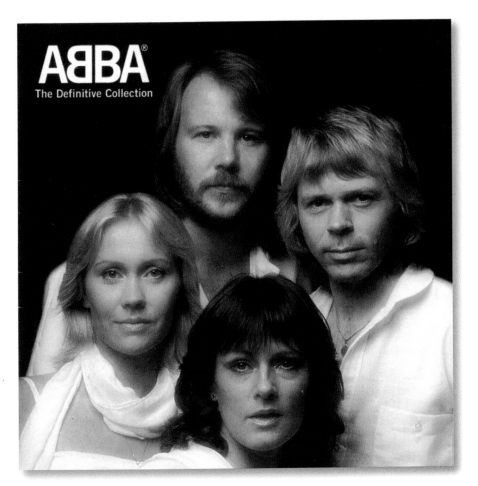

Under Attack
Thank You For The Music
Ring Ring remix (Anderson, Andersson, Cody, Sedaka, Ulvaeus)
Voulez-Vous Extended remix)
Highest chart position:
3 – Denmark, Korea

The singles

ABBA's singles are far too numerous to be listed in this book, so the following entries are those numbers that made it into the UK charts. All these songs were written and produced by Benny Andersson and Björn Ulvaeus unless otherwise stated.

Waterloo

(Anderson, Andersson, Ulvaeus)
B-side: *Watch Out*
Released on 20 April 1974, *Waterloo* was the winning entry for the Eurovision Song Contest earlier that month and made it to the Number 1 spot.

Ring Ring

(Anderson, Andersson, Ulvaeus)
B-side: *She's My Kind Of Girl*
Ring Ring had received moderate success in Sweden before it was released in the

UK. It made the Top 40 in the UK, peaking at Number 32.

I Do, I Do, I Do, I Do, I Do

(Anderson, Andersson, Ulvaeus)
B-side: *Rock Me*
Released on 12 July 1975, this firm favourite didn't fare as well as its predecessors, peaking in the UK charts at Number 38.

SOS

(Anderson, Andersson, Ulvaeus)
B-side: *Man In The Middle*
This was more like it! *SOS* – released on 20 September 1975 – climbed into the Top 10, reaching Number 6.

Mamma Mia

(Anderson, Andersson, Ulvaeus)
B-side: *Tropical Loveland*
Released on 13 December 1975, *Mamma Mia* gave ABBA their second Number 1 in the UK.

Fernando

(Anderson, Andersson, Ulvaeus)
B-side: *Hey, Hey, Helen*
This was also to prove a big hit for the group. It reached the Number 1 spot

in the charts following its release on 27 March 1976, and was to remain chart-bound for a total of fifteen weeks.

Dancing Queen
(Anderson, Andersson, Ulvaeus)
B-side: *That's Me*
Dancing Queen followed suit and reached Number 1, remaining in the UK charts for fifteen weeks. It was released on 21 August 1976. The song was then re-released on 5 September 1992. That time it peaked at Number 16 and remained in the charts for a total of five weeks.

Money, Money, Money
B-side: *Crazy World*
Peaking at Number 3, *Money, Money, Money* stayed in the charts for twelve weeks following its release on 20 November 1976.

Knowing Me, Knowing You
(Anderson, Andersson, Ulvaeus)
B-side: *Happy Hawaii*
Released on 26 February 1976, this track gave ABBA their fifth Number 1 in the UK charts. It remained in the charts for thirteen weeks.

The Name Of The Game
(Anderson, Andersson, Ulvaeus)
B-side: *I Wonder (Departure)*
Proving that ABBA could be taken seriously, this sixth Number 1 for the group stayed in the charts for a total of twelve weeks. The song was released on 22 October 1977.

Take A Chance On Me
B-side: *I'm A Marionette*
Released on 4 February 1978, *Take A Chance On Me* gave the group a seventh Number 1 in the UK charts. This was also the second time that ABBA had had three successive Number 1 hits. It remained in the charts for ten weeks.

Summer Night City
B-side: *Medley*
Summer Night City smouldered, but it didn't reach the Top 3 in the charts. It peaked at Number 5 and stayed in the charts for just nine weeks. The track was released on 16 September 1978.

Chiquitita
B-side: *Lovelight*
This soulful ballad was released on 3 February 1979 and peaked in the charts at Number 2, narrowly missing the top spot. It remained in the UK charts for a total of nine weeks.

Does Your Mother Know
B-side: *Kisses Of Fire*
This track was released as a single on 5 May 1979 and made it to Number 4. It stayed in the UK charts for nine weeks.

Angeleyes/Voulez-Vous
This double A-side made it to Number 3 in the UK and stayed in the charts for eleven weeks. The hit was released on 14 July 1979.

Gimme! Gimme! Gimme!
(A Man After Midnight)
B-side: *The King Has Lost His Crown*
Reaching Number 3 and remaining in the UK charts for twelve weeks, this song was released on 20 October 1979.

I Have A Dream
B-side: *Take A Chance On Me* (live)
The smooth, down-tempo *I Have A Dream* just missed the hot spot when it peaked at Number 2 following its release on 15 December 1979. It stayed in the UK charts for ten weeks.

The Winner Takes It All
B-side: *Elaine*
With some reference to Björn and Agnetha's recent divorce, this song took ABBA back to the Number 1 slot for their third round of successive chart-topping singles. The song remained in the charts for ten weeks following its release on 2 August 1980.

Super Trouper
B-side: *The Piper*
This title track from the album of the same name was also to provide the band with a Number 1 – it was their ninth time at the top of the UK charts. Released on 15 November 1980, the track remained in the charts for twelve weeks.

Lay All Your Love On Me
B-side: *On And On And On*
Released on 18 July 1981, *Lay All Your Love On Me* reached Number 7 in the UK and stayed in the charts for seven weeks.

One Of Us
B-side: *Should I Laugh Or Cry*
On 12 December 1981, the fact that the two couples' relationships were either breaking down or had broken down was epitomised in this sad single, with lead vocals by Agnetha. It peaked at Number 3 and remained in the charts for ten weeks.

Head Over Heels
B-side: *The Visitors*
Released on 20 February 1982, *Head Over Heels* reached the relatively lowly position of Number 25 and stayed in the charts for just seven weeks.

The Day Before You Came
B-side: *Cassandra*
Disappointingly, this track only made it to Number 32 in the singles charts, where it stayed for six weeks. It was released on 23 October 1982.

Under Attack
B-side: *You Owe Me One*
Under Attack fared slightly better than its predecessor when it made it to Number 26. It was released on 11 December 1982 and remained in the charts for eight weeks.

Thank You For The Music
B-side: *Our Last Summer*
The rousing *Thank You For The Music* proved an apt farewell to the

UK charts, peaking at Number 33. Following its release on 12 November 1983, it stayed in the charts for only six weeks.

The Money

Stig Anderson was an astute man and – whether it was through shrewdness, fluke or meticulous planning – he guided the four members of ABBA to fame and fortune with a single-minded devotion. Even those who were enthusiastic in Sweden didn't think that, once ABBA had won Eurovision, they could possibly go on to receive worldwide adoration – and the fortunes that went with it – after the elation of the contest had died down.

But they were wrong – very wrong. Anderson reportedly put £20 on ABBA to win, and he collected his £400 winnings on 7 April 1974. For him, ABBA winning the Eurovision wasn't the pinnacle of their careers – it was just the beginning. He had an extraordinary business acumen that saw him jetting off all over Europe to make deals for the release of ABBA records.

His quest to sign up the group with everyone he could was unusual. Normally, a group would make a deal with one major UK or US company, but that wasn't going to be enough for this curious businessman. He meticulously laid solid foundations between 1974 and 1975 that would make ABBA famous – and rich.

The philosophy wasn't simple and it certainly involved hard work – and tireless travelling and meetings – but it paid off. Rather than giving one major company the rights to ABBA, he used Polar Music to directly license the group to as many different countries as he possibly could. This meant a much greater financial gain from each deal and more commitment from the individual countries to sell ABBA records. It was to ultimately make them all millions.

But Anderson was a canny businessman, and even when ABBA became Sweden's largest export behind Volvo, he kept a tight rein on the finances and Polar Music continued to employ a moderate staff of fifty or so. But even in the 1970s and 1980s, the cost of living and taxes in Sweden were exceptionally high. The country has the

ABOVE
Spinning the
wheel, 1978

second highest tax rate in the world after Denmark. Even though each of the group was making a huge amount of money, much of it was disappearing. They were paying a whacking eighty-five per cent in tax.

The next idea was for the money to be invested to alleviate some of the tax, and it was used in business ventures to spread the risks. The company floated on

the stock exchange and each member of the group was liable for thirty-three per cent capital gains on share sales rather than paying the eighty-five per cent tax as a private individual. They set up the property company Badhus, which was to remain relatively successful. Then came Eastern Europe.

In lieu of cash, Anderson became involved in some strange commodities ranging from art treasures, rare coins, sports equipment and shirts to Polish potatoes. He believed that he was doing the right thing and that getting in behind the Iron Curtain was the way forward. In a misguided deal, some Iron Curtain record sales were partly paid for with Romanian oil that was imported through a Swedish company and sold on the Rotterdam spot market. The spot market collapsed and the value of ABBA oil drained away dramatically.

ABBA set up Pol Oil, which was to become the biggest mistake of their professional careers. It cost ABBA and Polar Music a fortune and caused a great deal of embarrassment and ultimately a huge falling-out that would see three members of the band lose their friendships with Anderson for good. Only Frida would remain in touch with their former manager.

With the collapse of the spot market in 1982, it was estimated that the company had spent $39 million buying up company shareholdings and by the end of the year equity accounted for only two per cent on the balance sheet. ABBA were in deep trouble. They had borrowed heavily because of spending money they didn't have and were near to financial collapse. Their subsequent company, Kuban, had its share dealings suspended by the Stockholm Stock Exchange and the band had one option: to sell up.

In another setback, the Swedish revenue discovered that three of the band members – Benny, Björn and Agnetha – had evaded tax payments of around £4.6 million relating to their business affairs. Frida had already sold her shares and was largely unaffected by the action. What that left each member of the band with financially is not clear. What is clear is that it was an ugly end to what had begun for ABBA as an exciting fairy tale – all in the pursuit of paying less tax.

BELOW Older and wiser, Benny and Björn, 2006

The Music Lives On –
The Abba Revival

More than two decades have passed since ABBA's "temporary break", when Benny and Björn focused their work on the musical *Chess*, and Agnetha and Frida decided to work on their solo careers. Rumours of a reunion, which have never gone away, resurfaced in late 2013 when there was talk of a 2014 reunion to mark the 40th anniversary of *Waterloo*. But Benny laid the rumours to rest when he said: "If any one of us has opened the door a crack, I'm shutting it now."

Despite the lack of ABBA in the flesh, though, the music has lived on in the form of the musical *Mamma Mia!*, the stunningly successful film of the musical and a multitude of tribute bands such as Björn Again. Not only that, the 1990s saw the beginning of a major revival in the music of ABBA with a number of hit films including *Muriel's Wedding* using the group's music on their soundtracks.

In addition, the compilation CD *ABBA Gold*, first released in 1992 has sold more than twenty-eight million copies. The follow-up, *More ABBA Gold*, first released a year later, has sold more than three million worldwide. They were followed in 1994 by box sets like *Thank You For The Music* that have included the greatest hits as well as rare and previously unreleased recordings.

When the hugely successful *Mamma Mia!* celebrated its fifth anniversary in April 2004 in London's West End, the performance was attended by Frida, Benny and Björn. In Sweden, the premiere for the musical (which opened in February 2004) was attended by all four members of the group. And in July 2008, the members

of the group got together at the Swedish premiere of the *Mamma Mia!* Film. They used the occasion to deny that they would ever reunite.

Universal Music, which eventually bought out Polygram (the owner of the original Polar Music), has strived to keep the ABBA story alive. The label has continually upgraded the ABBA catalogue and the eight original studio albums: *Ring Ring*, *Waterloo*, *ABBA*, *Arrival*, *ABBA – The Album*, *Voulez-Vous*, *Super Trouper* and *The Visitors* have all been reissued. Each original album's re-release included additional bonus tracks packaged in revised artwork and accompanied by a comprehensive booklet. In 2004, Universal released a new *Waterloo* that came with a DVD of previously unreleased television performances to mark the thirtieth anniversary of the album.

The company have also reissued the compilation albums *ABBA Gold* and *ABBA Oro* – the latter for the South American market – with revised booklets and updated notes. There is also a double CD that gathers together all of ABBA's singles. *The Definitive*

Collection was ranked at number 180 in *Rolling Stone* magazine's five hundred best albums of all time. In 2005, Universal released a box set entitled *The Complete Studio Recordings*.

There are now two different DVDs of ABBA's videos: *The Definitive Collection* and *ABBA Gold*. Both include remastered original film clips.

In addition, the two live concert films, *ABBA – The Movie* and *ABBA in Concert*, have been restored and re-released on DVD with previously unseen material. Universal has also released *Super Trouper*, an official documentary, and *The Last Video*, a short film featuring all group members making cameo appearances.

In early 2012 came news that fans had been longing to hear: *The Visitors*, the band's final studio album, would be reissued in a deluxe edition with bonus tracks and a DVD of rare footage, in April. What's more, the reissue included a previously unheard song: *From a Twinkling Star to a Passing Angel*, recorded in 1981.

Björn Again –
A tribute

I n 1988, Melbourne in Australia was the setting for what seemed at the time an unlikely concept: an ABBA tribute band. The idea worked and now, more than twenty years later, the band Björn Again are still going strong and are as popular as ever. Indeed it turned out to be such a good idea that many, many ABBA tribute bands earn a decent living.

The idea was the brainchild of Rod Leissle and John Tyrrell, who renamed themselves Benny Anderwear and Björn Volvo-us. Together with female band members known as Agnetha Falstart and Frida Longstokin, they formed Björn Again and made their debut at The Tote in Melbourne in 1989. The crowd went wild for the band, who not only looked like ABBA but also sounded uncannily like them.

Today, in fact, there are five Björn Again tribute bands and they have

played in more than seventy countries. They are managed by Rod Leissle and his management company with offices in Australia, the UK and North America.

Within two years of forming, Björn Again played in Gothenburg, where they received a telegram from Björn Ulvaeus reading: "The best of luck. Anyone who looks like me ought to have a successful career!" Although the man himself was impressed with the stage show that Björn Again were putting on, he was not so enamoured with their 'Swedish' accents. In 1992 he stated on Belfast

BELOW Björn Again – London

Radio: "I am flattered by everything except Björn Again's accents. I hope my accent isn't as lousy!"

What a twenty-nine-year-old man was doing rooting around in his wardrobe is anybody's guess, but Rod Leissle decided – upon finding some old flared trousers and platform shoes – to listen again to 1970s music. He got listening to ABBA and was suddenly struck with the idea of putting on a stage show that would recreate the era with its catchy music and outrageous fashion. His belief was that the Swedish band "globally encapsulated all that was good", and that ABBA were the ideal 70s phenomenon on which to base his slightly crazy idea.

But his notion was to prove almost as much of a phenomenon as ABBA themselves. Nearly forty years after ABBA first came to international attention, Björn Again are still thriving as the tribute band that followed in the footsteps of the original group who took the world by storm.

The 1980s, with its various new musical genres, left ABBA, as a pure pop group, struggling against the competition. By 1987 they were generally considered to have passed their prime. That, combined with tensions within the group and the breakdown of both marriages, left ABBA with few places to go professionally. But within two years they would be back – their tribute band would spend the months between 1988 and 1989 searching for theatrical ideas to make an exciting stage show exciting while rehearsing music and auditioning singers for Agnetha's and Frida's roles. It caused a major revolution in the music industry, and there followed widespread revival and nostalgia.

Following some sell-out concerts in Melbourne, Björn Again toured Australia, and were featured on several national television shows. The band were quickly establishing themselves as a cult band and in 1990 they continued an extensive tour which led to them becoming household names in every state across the country.

Having gained a wide following in their home country, the tribute band set off for Sweden, and 1991 saw them maintaining a hectic touring schedule. It was around this time that Björn Again employed Paul Franklin as their agent.

In 1992 *ABBA Gold* was released on

LEFT London – Family Prom in the Park

BJÖRN AGAIN – A TRIBUTE

RIGHT
Björn Again –
Australia

CD – the first time the band had been released on the latest technology – and, in the run-up to its release, Björn Again were invited to perform on national television in Sweden. The reception they received was extraordinary, and they next undertook an extensive tour of Europe, including Scandinavia. The tour took in the UK's *Jonathan Ross Show*, the Reading Festival and seven consecutive sell-out shows at the Town and Country Club (now the Forum) in London. They went on to perform *Dancing Queen* with U2 in Stockholm.

The same year, the real Benny and Björn invited Björn Again to meet them on their visit to Stockholm. The band then found huge critical acclaim on the UK's university circuit and played their first gig at the Royal Albert Hall, where the concert was, once again, a sell-out.

In 1994, the Australian hit movie *Muriel's Wedding* included a number of ABBA songs and director PJ Hogan invited Björn Again to perform live at the Cannes Film Festival. The band then played at London's Gay Pride to an audience of more than three hundred thousand before embarking on their first North American tour. It was not

long before the band had played their thousandth concert, and the following year saw them touring once again in Australia, North America, the UK and Europe.

In 1996, Björn Again began a gruelling tour around the UK before starting a world tour that saw them performing in, among other countries, Hong Kong, Japan and Ireland. The trip to Hong Kong was particularly memorable for the band as they were invited to play at the Royal Hong Kong Yacht Club as part of the official celebrations when Hong Kong was handed back to China.

To mark their tenth anniversary in 1998, Björn Again were back at the Royal Albert Hall for a sell-out show before making an appearance at the Gay Games in Amsterdam. They were the support act for the Spice Girls on two occasions before beginning yet another UK tour. The following year saw them open at the Glastonbury Festival, where they were a huge success.

Next came a 'fly on the wall' documentary broadcast by Channel 5 that went on to win a coveted Rose D'or TV award in Montreux. The

band then celebrated 150 years of Harrods with owner Mohammed Al Fayed. Björn Again saw in the new millennium with three parties including a private function with Rowan Atkinson, a street party in Belfast and a show in Newcastle. The last year of the millennium was also the year the *Mamma Mia!* stage show opened in London's West End.

Fans of Björn Again demanded more tours and the New Year was to see the band set off on tours in the UK, the rest of Europe and North America (three tours were running simultaneously). The band also performed at the launch of Chinese television channel CCTV, being watched by an estimated one billion people worldwide. The following three years were just as busy with appearances at London's Hyde Park with Shania Twain and a concert to mark the New Year at the Millennium Dome. They went on to support the American singer a year later on her own tour.

The loss in 2004 of tour manager and sound enginer Malcolm Kingsnorth was devastating for the band, and they held a benefit concert in his honour with Billy Connolly and

LEFT London – Family Prom in the Park

other household names. Björn Again also went on tour with Cher in 2004 and played at Russell Crowe's wedding. Highlights from 2006 included being invited by Jasper Carrott to perform at his Rock With Laughter as well as performing at JK Rowling's Masquerade Ball in aid of Scotland's MS Society. In May 2007, Björn Again played once again at The Tote in Melbourne to celebrate their eighteenth anniversary as a touring band.

The next four years saw a steady flow of work across the world, and in 2010 a fifty-date UK tour called Here We Go Again celebrated twenty years of the band and looked forward to the next twenty. The show responded to the success of the *Mamma Mia!* Film by picking up on parts of the theme and content. And in 2011, Björn Again are as busy as they ever were.

Mamma Mia!

The records just keep stacking up. The film version of *Mamma Mia!*, adapted from the 1999 London musical of the same name and based on the music of ABBA, keeps rewriting the record books the way the group did in the music industry of the 1970s.

The film, which stars Meryl Streep, Pierce Brosnan, Colin Firth and Stellan Skarsgård, has grossed $609,841,637 in box offices worldwide, and along the way has become the most successful British-made film of all time. It is also the third highest-grossing film ever in British box offices, and in terms of worldwide takings it is the highest-grossing musical in history. In the United States and Canada, *Mamma Mia!* broke the record for the highest-grossing opening weekend for a musical.

In short, *Mamma Mia! The Movie* is a phenomenon, much like the stage version, which has now been seen by more than forty-five million people across the world. The stage musical has been performed well over five thousand times in London since it opened in 1999; it is the eleventh longest-running Broadway musical of all time; and it is reckoned that on any day, there are at least seven productions running in theatres around the world.

The show was, of course, named after ABBA's chart-topper of 1975. Playwright Catherine Johnson teamed up with Benny Andersson and Björn Ulvaeus to create something truly unique, and the story those first theatregoers witnessed in 1999 revolves around a young girl named Sophie. She lives on a Greek island with her mother, Donna, and is about to marry her fiancé Sky. She wants her father to walk down the aisle with her – but she doesn't know who he is. Donna, who runs the local taverna, is reluctant to talk to her daughter about the past.

Undeterred, Sophie discovers an old diary, which describes three dates her mother went on with different men. Without her mother's knowledge, she invites all three men to her

forthcoming wedding.

All three men arrive. Harry is a banker with an interesting laugh, while Bill is typically Australian. Sam had an affair with Donna twenty years previously, despite being engaged to someone else. For her part, Donna invites two old friends (Rosie and Tanya), who used to sing with her in Donna and the Dynamos, to come to her daughter's wedding.

Donna has already told Sophie that the taverna was built with money that came from an inheritance. Sophie is also told that she is named after the benefactor, Sophia, who is Bill's aunt. It is natural for Sophie to assume that Bill is her father, and she asks him to give her away. However, after some confusion and mix-ups, the other two potential fathers believe that they will be giving their 'daughter' away.

Meanwhile, Sophie writes them all notes to say that Donna will give

ABOVE A fifth anniversary show in London, 2004

RIGHT More from the fifth anniversary show

Sophie and Sky then announce to their wedding guests that they have decided not to marry for the time being. Donna and Sam decide to wed instead, while Rosie and Bill become mutually attracted. Harry is happy to divulge that he is gay and in a relationship, while Sophie and Sky decide to travel the world.

Throughout the entire stage production, audience participation is a prerequisite and with the inclusion of *Dancing Queen, The Winner Takes It All, SOS, Knowing Me, Knowing You, Take A Chance On Me, I Do, I Do, I Do, I Do, I Do, The Name Of The Game, Money, Money, Money, Super Trouper, Gimme! Gimme! Gimme! (A Man After Midnight)* and *Mamma Mia,* not many theatregoers can resist joining in. The other ABBA songs included in the musical are *Honey, Honey, Thank You For The Music, Chiquitita, Lay All Your Love On Me, Does Your Mother Know, I Have A Dream, Voulez-Vous* and, of course, *Waterloo.*

The first *Mamma Mia!* premiered in London's Prince Edward Theatre on 6 April 1999, while on Broadway the show took to the stage on 18 October 2001 at the Winter Garden Theatre. In Canada, *Mamma Mia!* was launched at

her away. However, she and Sky are wondering whether they know each other well enough to marry after all. Sam and Donna have a bitter row over Sophie's parentage during which it becomes apparent to them both that they are still deeply in love.

The wedding day arrives – and bride and groom decide to proceed with the nuptials – and it is made obvious that Sophie's paternity cannot be proved. All decide that it doesn't matter and all three men wish to remain a part of her life.

the Royal Alexandra Theatre in Toronto on 23 May 2000. In London, the show transferred to the Prince of Wales Theatre in 2004 – and it is still running there. With 1,500 performances on 15

May 2005, the musical beat records set by *The Sound Of Music* and *The King And I* and by September 2006 had become the longest running musical on Broadway. It had already become the

longest running musical in Las Vegas – a record which it set with its 1,000th performance in June 2005.

So who are the driving forces behind such huge hits of stage and screen? For Benny and Björn, a meeting with Sir Tim Rice planted the seeds for writing a musical. While still members of ABBA, the duo co-wrote *Chess* with Sir Tim, and it opened in London's West End in 1986. A year earlier, Benny and Björn had seen their first musical, *Kristina Från Duvemåla*, open in Sweden. The show ran for three years and then in 2002, *Chess* began its own run in Stockholm.

Catherine Johnson, who already had a string of plays to her name, wrote the entertaining, feelgood story, which is interspersed with the musical contributions of Benny and Björn, and came up with the screenplay for the film. Johnson, who is responsible for successful plays like *Rag Doll, Renegades, Shang-a-Lang, Little Baby Nothing* and *Too Much Too Young,* has won a number of awards, including the Thames Television's Writer-In-Residence Award and Thames Television's Best Play Award. In 2002, Johnson was nominated for a Tony Award for her book for *Mamma Mia!*

The idea of using ABBA's music, but in an original musical, was the brainchild of producer Judy Craymer. She began her career in the theatre with the Haymarket Theatre in Leicester before working on the original production of *Cats* with Cameron Mackintosh in 1981. The following year, Craymer joined Sir Tim Rice's production company, Heartaches, before becoming managing director of Three Knights in 1984. Her career then took her into film and television – including *White Mischief* and *Madame Souzatzka* – before she teamed up with Benny and Björn to form Littlestar Services in 1996 along with Richard East. The idea? To produce the stage show *Mamma Mia!*

This was the second time that Craymer had worked with Benny and Björn, and she went on to become executive producer of *The Winner Takes It All,* an official documentary about ABBA. Craymer is also executive producer of *Super Troupers: A Celebratory Film From 'Waterloo' To 'Mamma Mia!'* as well as the global producer for the musical. Her work with *Mamma Mia!* won her the Woman of the Year Award in 2002.

The original London production was directed by Phyllida Lloyd and featured choreography by Anthony Van Laast. Among the original cast were Siobhán McCarthy, Lisa Stokke and Hilton McRae. The critics were ecstatic, and reviews included "Fresh and exhilarating" from the *Sunday Express* while the *Daily Mail* described it as "Sheer enjoyability – a five star performance". Charles Spencer of the *Daily Telegraph* said the show was "The perfect ticket for a feel-good night out" while *The Guardian* described the experience as " … great fun".

Reviews from the other side of the Atlantic were equally appreciative, with Matt Wolf of Associated Press announcing that it was "Quite simply a phenomenon!" His praise was echoed by *The Today Show* in Australia, which said

LEFT Mamma Mia! in New York

it was "The best night out you'll ever have". Perhaps the highest praise came from David Sinclair at *The Times*, who said *Mamma Mia!* was "A production of tremendous warmth, vitality and technical excellence that offers an evening of unbridled fun. It is a tribute to the scriptwriting skill of Catherine Johnson that the ABBA songs are slotted so naturally into the storyline. While being swept along by the ingenious choreography and witty dialogue, I found myself examining ABBA's music in a new light."

In all, the stage show of Mamma Mia! has been performed in thirteen languages besides English – Danish, Dutch, Flemish, French, German, Indonesian, Italian, Japanese, Korean, Norwegian, Portuguese, Russian, Spanish and Swedish – and has spread throughout the world. The latest news of its global reach came when the Chinese got their own version, which debuted at Shanghai's Grand Theatre in July 2011.

But *Mamma Mia!* first hit the United States at the Orpheum Theatre in San Francisco, opening on 17 November 2000 and running for three months before moving on to Los Angeles. It stayed at the city's Shubert Theatre until May 2001, when it moved to the Cadillac Palace in Chicago. After three months in the Windy City, the production made its New York debut – at the Winter Garden Theatre on Broadway – on 18 October 2001. It is still there, directed by Phyllida Lloyd and featuring the choreography of Anthony Van Laast.

The Broadway production is far from the only production in the United States, though. The Las Vegas production ran for six years, from February 2003 until January 2009, along the way becoming the longest-running Broadway/West End musical in the 'Entertainment Capital of the World'. Elsewhere in North America, the Lloyd/Van Laast *Mamma Mia!* had a five-year run at Toronto's Royal Alexandra Theatre, closing in May 2005.

The show has been performed on countless tours across the world and, besides the major cities already mentioned, has had permanent European productions in Antwerp, Barcelona, Berlin, Gothenburg, Hamburg, Madrid, Milan, Moscow, Stockholm, Stuttgart and Utrecht. Elsewhere in the world, permanent

productions have entertained in Daegu, Fukuoka, Mexico, Nagoya, Osaka, Seongnam, Seoul and Tokyo. All of this extraordinary success compares favourably with the global acclaim accorded to *Mamma Mia! The Movie*, which, as we have seen, has overwhelmed box offices the world over.

Not that the critics have always been kind about the film, and some have reserved special scorn for the singing efforts of its stars. While Meryl Streep, who plays Donna, received plaudits for her vocal skills, the same cannot be said for Pierce Brosnan, who filled the role of Sam. The *Miami Herald* rather ungallantly likened his voice to that of "a wounded raccoon", while another critic wondered in print whether Brosnan was being subjected to a prostate examination while the cameras were turning.

But Brosnan was happy to be involved. He is reported to have had no idea what the film was about when he signed up; the producers had merely told him it was being filmed in Greece and Meryl Streep was in it. He would have signed for anything involving Streep ("that gorgeous blonde I fancied terribly

LEFT
Sir Cameron Mackintosh attends the Royal Charity Gala Performance of the musical Mamma Mia!, 2004

MAMMA MIA!

RIGHT
Mamma Mia!, a
must for all ABBA
fans

in drama school"), he declared.

In the main, critics were kind when the film was released in the UK on 30 June 2008, and cinemagoers were wildly enthusiastic. And a few days later, on July 4, all four members of ABBA were photographed together for the first time since 1986, as they gathered at the film's Swedish premiere in Stockholm. That occasion really fuelled the rumours of a reunion.

The film – made with a budget of $52 million – marked the movie directorial debut of Phyllida Lloyd, who thus followed on from her success with stage productions of *Mamma Mia!* Benny Andersson and Björn Ulvaeus were involved as producers, as were Judy Craymer and actors Tom Hanks and Rita Wilson. The screenplay was written by – who else? – Catherine Johnson, who rejigged some of the stage show's musical content along the way.

Besides Streep and Brosnan, the cast included the young American actress and singer-songwriter Amanda Seyfried, who played Sophie, Colin Firth (Harry), the Swedish actor Stellan Skarsgård (Bill), Dominic Cooper (Sky), Julie Walters, Christine Baranski, Philip

Michael, Ashley Lilley, Rachel McDowall, Enzo Squillino and Niall Buggy. And guess which musical pair make cameo appearances, as a pianist during the *Dancing Queen* sequence and as a Greek god during the closing credits? Yes, that would be the unmistakeable figures of Benny and Björn.

Filming started in August 2007 on the Greek island of Skopelos – where a temporary beach bar and jetty were built – and the village of Damouchari on the mainland. Other locations used in the film included the Lloyds building in London, while some song and dance numbers were shot on a new stage at Pinewood Studios.

The soundtrack album of the film, released in 2008, was another massive success – it has sold more than five million copies throughout the world. And the DVD has ousted the likes of *Titanic* and *Pirates of the Caribbean: The Curse of the Black Pearl* from the top of the UK best-sellers list. It is thought that one UK household in every four has a copy of the film.

The film has had so much success, in short, that the inevitable rumours of a sequel have surfaced from time to time.

There are certainly enough hit songs in the ABBA back catalogue for a winning storyline to be constructed and for the project to be another sing-along success, but firm news of a new production has been hard to come by. Universal Studios boss David Linde seemed keen on the idea in 2008, as he watched all that money roll through the world's box offices, but according to Amanda Seyfried in early 2011, "that's never going to happen … How would they get all the actors back?"

There can be no doubt, however, that a sequel would be welcomed by vast armies of ABBA and cinema fans worldwide.

Thank You For The Music

While the four members of the band continue to work, live and play apart and the wished-for reunion is still a figment of promoters' fevered imaginations, fans have plenty of opportunities to keep their hunger for all things ABBA satisfied. Any number of CDs and DVDs can be revisited any time a fan wishes; *Mamma Mia!*, with its instant reminders of Benny and Björn's music, can still be seen on stages and in cinemas across the world; and, if that's not enough, an exhibition dedicated to the memory of the much-loved group is touring throughout the world.

ABBAWorld, an interactive exhibition filled with music, original costumes, images, instruments and memorabilia, has been on show in London, Melbourne, Sydney, Györ in Hungary and Prague in the Czech Republic – and the plans don't stop there. Delays in the opening of ABBA the Museum in Stockholm, due to "project complications" and setbacks in the renovation of its base building, resulted in the organisers taking the show on the road.

Featuring more than 750 pieces of memorabilia, ABBAWorld is officially approved by Anni-Frid, Agnetha, Benny and Björn, who supplied most of the exhibits. It is produced by Stockholm company Touring Exhibitions, Polar Music, Synerga and Eventum Exhibitions.

As the tour set out on the road in 2009, Touring Exhibitions president Magnus Danielsson said: "It's perfect for the whole family, with so much to see, hear, feel, touch and experience, thanks to state-of-the-art technology. [ABBAWorld] will even enable you to

virtually to sing and perform ABBA's hits in front of a live sell-out crowd at stadiums where ABBA performed back in the day."

And Björn Ulvaeus added: "ABBAWorld is going places where we never had a chance to play when we were still active as a group, and that's great."

Meanwhile, you just can't keep those reunion rumours down. The speculation restarts whenever and

wherever former ABBA members
turn up in public together, as Agnetha
and Anni-Frid did in 2009 when they
accepted a Swedish music industry
lifetime achievement award on behalf
of the group. There was another double

act appearance in New York in 2010,
when Anni-Frid and Benny represented
the group as they were finally inducted
into the Rock and Roll Hall of Fame.

Agnetha became the latest to fuel the
reunion rumour fire when she let slip to

LEFT Benny, Frida and Björn at the fifth anniversary performance

consider a one-off reunion, maybe for a good cause."

But it would have to be a *very* good cause, it seems. It has been revealed that the group were offered $1 billion, in return for which they would play a hundred-date world tour, in 2000. They turned it down. Björn said at the time: "This is the budget of a small country, so we had to give it some thought. In the end we decided that, whatever offer was on the table, it would be stupid to reform and utterly ludicrous to change the images people all over the world have of us."

And Benny added: "We'd need a good reason to reform, and I just don't see one. We could never recreate the old days. I'd rather be remembered for the way we were thirty years ago."

Even flat denials like that are not enough to stop the reunion theorists, who even went so far as to suggest the group could have got together for the marriage of Prince William and Kate Middleton in April 2011.

Perhaps now would be a good time to lay the rumours to rest, say "Thank you for the music" and let ABBA's glorious music speak for itself.

a Swedish magazine in 2011: "I just feel it would be fun to meet, chat about the old days and perhaps perform together. We would not get together again for a tour like the Rolling Stones and other old bands do. I think we would all

ALSO AVAILABLE IN THE LITTLE BOOK SERIES

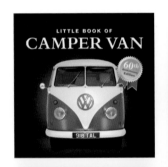

ALSO AVAILABLE IN THE LITTLE BOOK SERIES

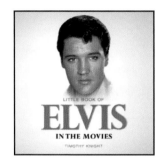

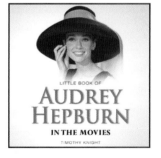

**The pictures in this book were
provided courtesy of the following:**

GETTY IMAGES
101 Bayham Street, London NW1 0AG

Design and artwork by Scott Giarnese

Published by G2 Entertainment Limited

Publishers: Jules Gammond and Edward Adams